DANTE, MICHELANGELO
AND MILTON

DANTE
MICHELANGELO
AND MILTON

by

JOHN ARTHOS

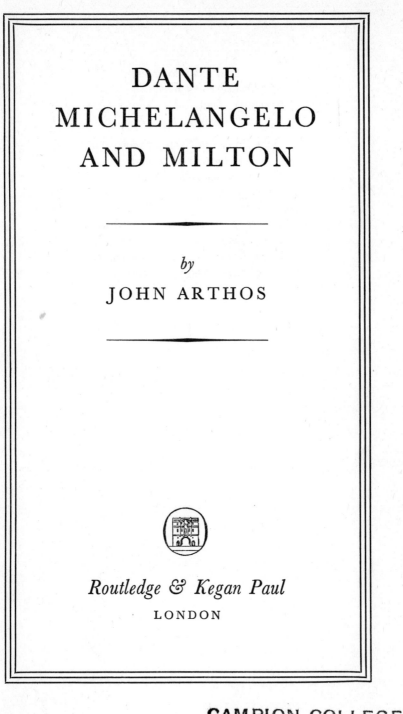

Routledge & Kegan Paul
LONDON

First published 1963
by Routledge and Kegan Paul Ltd
Broadway House, 68–74 Carter Lane
London, E.C.4

Printed in Great Britain
in the City of Oxford
at the Alden Press

To
M.L.J.J.M.

CONTENTS

PREFACE

IT IS ALWAYS A PLEASURE to return to Saintsbury and to discover again the judgments one would not know how to improve
on. His praise of the ancient treatise *On the Sublime* remains as
fresh as it is just—'it abides in thought alone as in history, and
almost all deserves to be written in letters of gold'. And when he
came to that sentence in it he was never tired of praising,
'Beautiful words are the very light of thought', he extended its
meaning to express his own central conviction, 'These words
themselves are the lantern of criticism'. I am therefore under-
standably encouraged in using Longinus's work as the starting
point of an effort to characterize the effect of greatness in
three of the most remarkable writers in modern literature.

Saintsbury valued the force of Longinus's mind, its power to
penetrate and systematize, and its boldness in advancing
towards conclusions even Aristotle held back from. Longinus
took the great writers of antiquity as the standard of excellence,
and he held up their greatness, by whatever means communicated and in whatever forms—prose, verse, drama—as what
mattered most, and what would continue to matter to all men,
in whatever society, who had a proper reverence for nobility of
mind and beauty of expression. Longinus, indeed, made it no
small part of his purpose to argue that the greatest effects of
literature depend on a harmony of excellences, of mind and
character and language, and perfections of technique could not
of themselves attain the success serious men value most.

All this—so nobly and persuasively put—was reinforced by
what we must call genius, observations on particular works
hardly less than miraculous in their justice. His praise of Homer

ix

as of Plato, his rescue of one of the great Sappho odes, the unfailing discrimination, all inspire such confidence in us that, as Saintsbury said, we would even submit Shakespeare to him with little fear, and be sure that he would understand the greatness of Dante. He holds before us the great examples of antiquity and he values them, not because they fit the prescriptions of certain rules or satisfy the conditions of genre, but because they succeed in discovering and following the forms that were theirs of necessity, and because they are true to the central traditions of civilization at its best. Nor was he bound by the limits of particular cultures, and he could bring the author of *Genesis* to stand beside Homer and Plato as testimony of the magnificence of mind and expression to which all men worthy of the name must respond.

Generations have discussed the propriety of the use of the word 'sublime' in place of what would more literally be translated as 'elevated', but the idea of the sublime—that which is elevated in mind and also religiously—is in fact what is always leading him on. It is true that with Kant and Burke the idea becomes less clear and in some ways at least it is of dubious usefulness, but Longinus's conception of sublimity is not vague and it is sustained by arguments that we must continue to honour. After him it is only Coleridge, I believe, who does justice to the value of the idea.

Longinus believed that the basis of the power of literature was the enlargement and strengthening of the understanding. We have often lost sight of this because we have been so eager to recognize his originality in placing the emphasis he does upon the importance of ecstasy, or transport, an emphasis we particularly value because it is at the heart of his rejection of all those critics who make rules and devices and figures the matter of most consequence in the judgment of literature. And because, as I see it, the balance needs to be righted, I have thought it proper to begin this work with a study of Longinus that attempts to do that, and at the same time to outline the philosophical context of his position. It is, in fact, only when this is understood that we are able to submit to him 'without fear' the superlative accomplishments of later times.

There are many works of literature that lead us to think about them as Longinus speaks of the greatest works of antiquity, and

it is in certain respects arbitrary to single out Dante, Michelangelo and Milton in order to test the scope and value of
Longinus's reasoning and to use it to help us understand the
greatness of their achievements. These are, of course, among the
greatest names we know, and although Michelangelo is more
valued for his work in other arts than in literature it has become
increasingly clear of recent years that his poetry is of the highest
quality and that on occasion it shares in the power and marvel
of the rest. What makes them all equally interesting, however,
in the light of Longinus's criticism, is the effort each of them
makes to relate works of art to divine principles. It is indeed
because Longinus also believed that the effect of sublime
language was to raise the listener 'near to the mighty mind
of God' that there is a special persuasion to measure their
reasoning by his, and to submit their works to be judged by
the standards he articulates and so superbly justifies.

Dante, Michelangelo and Milton believed that works of art
could be religiously inspired, and, like Longinus, they rested
in the conviction that poetry depended on truth. All of them
took much trouble to explain what they considered to be the
relation of the work of the artist to the truths of philosophy and
religion, and at particular points the thought of each of them
approached close enough to the position of Longinus to enable
us to make the final discriminations. What their theories have
to do with their achievements and how far these bear Longinus
out is the subject of this study.

I am happy here to acknowledge my dependence on W.
Rhys Roberts's text and translation of Longinus, but from time
to time I make use of the readings of W. H. Fyfe, G. M. A.
Grube, and Augusto Rostagni. I quote almost always from the
Carlyle-Wicksteed translation of Dante, and the J. A. Symonds
translation of Michelangelo.

I am also glad to acknowledge the permission of the *University
of Toronto Quarterly* to reprint part of an essay on Dante that
first appeared there. And I must also express my gratitude to the
Guggenheim Foundation, the American Philosophical Society,
and the Horace H. Rackham School of Graduate Studies of
the University of Michigan for funds that have enabled me to
complete this work.

LONGINUS AND THE
SUBLIME

––––––––

FOR LONGINUS the mind that is elevated by language is rich
with joy and passion and the sense of the power of thought. He
speaks often of transport and rapture, and there is no doubt
that by the value he sets on vehement emotion he risks the
interpretation that passion and even rage are the substance of
the greatest poetry, but he warns us against any such reading of
his argument in the one telling way, by asserting the primacy of
thought even in ecstasy: of the several conditions necessary
for the achievement of the sublime, elevation of mind holds the
foremost rank (IX, 1). He always returns to this, that the
satisfaction of the mind is the finally important requirement.

And if this is his ultimate emphasis, he supports it by an
affirmation that is equally pervasive in the treatise—the
values of poetry and oratory at their best are known to be such
only by men of well-balanced nature: the ethical forming of the
poet and orator, and of their audience, is the necessary basis of
the mind that aspires to elevated thought. 'You must know,
my dear friend', he writes, 'that it is with the sublime as in the
common life of man. In life nothing can be considered great
which it is held great to despise. For instance, riches, honours,
distinctions, sovereignties, and all other things which possess
in abundance the external trappings of the stage, will not
seem, to a man of sense, to be supreme blessings, since the very
contempt of them is reckoned good in no small degree, and in
any case those who could have them, but are high-souled
enough to disdain them, are more admired than those who have

them. So also in the case of sublimity in poems and prose writings, we must consider whether some supposed examples have not simply the appearance of elevation with many idle accretions, so that when analysed they are found to be mere vanity—objects which a noble nature will rather despise than admire. For, as if instinctively, our soul is uplifted by the true sublime; it takes a proud flight, and is filled with joy and vaunting, as though it had itself produced what it has heard' (VII, 1–2).

Longinus appears further to believe that the very principles that lead to the attainment of the effect of sublimity are those that also effect order and harmony in the individual: 'There inhere in all things by nature certain constituents which are part and parcel of their substance. It must needs be, therefore, that we shall find one source of the sublime in the systematic selection of the most important elements, and the power of forming, by their mutual combination, what may be called one body' (X, 1). Which is as much as to say—he is here speaking of Sappho and Homer—that the unity of the poem depends on the balance of passions in the author and in the disposition to that same balance in the very concourse of passions in the reader.

Longinus gains much of his authority by not losing himself in philosophizing. In philosophy there is always the premise that reason with its abstractions will present us as a system a complete analogy to a man. But Longinus allows us to listen to him with our senses as well as with our mind, he gives us the order rather than a theory of humanity, and this, so to speak, does us an honour—it allows us to be ourselves, to waive our ignorance and to rely upon our nature. This does not mean that he is not philosophical, or that he does not have fixed principles. On the contrary, he is intent on the declaration of basic principles as everywhere the foundation of sound criticism, and most especially he declares again and again that the ascendancy of thought must never be sacrificed to the allure of feeling. It is indeed this affirmation that supports his notion of the harmony that exists in nature as well as in art, the necessary dominance of thought.

He gives perhaps equal emphasis to the necessity of nobility in the character of the poet. This requirement may ultimately depend on the writer's own commitments, whether as a Stoic or a Platonist, although often enough it may be sufficiently acceptable as a commonplace. But if there is anything that would lead us to inquire more deeply into the philosophy that underlies his arguing it would be the stress he places on the relation of poetry to the divine, a stress that is not that of a simple religiousness as it is in Pindar, who is also intent on the nature of the elevation of the greatest poetry; with Longinus it is everywhere certain that his religiousness is supported by reason. It would be well if one could sort out anything approaching a system of ideas in this reasoning for it would teach us how, in accepting so happily his judgments, we are also being induced to share in his commitments. And if this should become clear, we should be in a better position to understand how to apply his idea of the nature of sublimity to the achievements of the Middle Ages and the Renaissance.

Perhaps the most significant notion of Longinus's criticism is that a reader of poetry is rather easily raised to an elevated state (II, 2; VII, 2; XIII, 2). This idea in its turn depends on recognizing the similarity of the process by which the reader of poetry cultivates his mind with that in which poetry is composed. Longinus says clearly that sublime works are products of art as well as of nature, that infinite pains have gone to their making. He also supposes that the reader of a poem, like the poet, has led a life in which he has given continuous thought and care to his own cultivation and integrity: ' ... the truly eloquent must be free from low and ignoble thoughts. For it is not possible that men with mean and servile ideas and aims prevailing throughout their lives should produce anything that is admirable and worthy of immortality' (IX, 3). This means that on one side the intricacies of art, on the other the intricacies of cultivation come together, and at any moment the fire may be struck: 'Sublimity flashing forth at the right moment scatters everything before it like a thunderbolt' (I, 4). I do not think he means to say that we live at such a pitch that we are always looking forward to the next instant to be kindled into enthusiasm. He merely means that we are always conscious of the life without us, its complexity is always understood, and that our consciousness is alive and alert: 'We must, therefore,

... although we have to do rather with an endowment than with an acquirement, nurture our souls (as far as that is possible) to thoughts sublime, and make them always pregnant, so to say, with noble inspiration' (IX, 1). 'Nature has appointed us men to be no base or ignoble animals; but when she ushers us into life and into the vast universe as into some great assembly, to be as it were spectators of the mighty whole and the keenest aspirants for honour, forthwith she implants in our souls the unconquerable love of whatever is elevated and more divine than we. Wherefore not even the entire universe suffices for the thought and contemplation within the reach of the human mind, but our imaginations often pass beyond the bounds of space, and if we survey our life on every side and see how much more it everywhere abounds in what is striking, and great, and beautiful, we shall soon discern the purpose of our birth' (XXXV, 2–3). And again: 'All other qualities prove their possessors to be men, but sublimity raises them near the majesty of God' (XXXVI, 1).

If aspiration towards the divine and the satisfaction of contemplation arise from the nature of man, and if those who succeed in expressing what they have seen are able to bring us into a state like their own, this might end in the cult of an undefined enthusiasm if there were not the clearest emphasis on the necessity of nobility in the nature of the poet. And nobility for Longinus means not only greatness of soul, it means purity, rectitude, the honouring of truth, generosity, and the reverence due to the gods: 'Much superior to the passages respecting the Battle of the Gods [in Homer] are those which represent the divine nature as it really is—pure and great and undefiled' (IX, 8). 'Sublimity is the true ring of a noble mind' (IX, 2), and men must own an integrity as perfect as that of Plato's philosopher: 'Nothing can be considered great which it is a sign of greatness to despise' (VII, 1).

In short, the mind of the poet has been nurtured in honouring truth. Longinus is careful to distinguish between the aims of poetry and oratory: in the first the fabulous has its scope, in the other, in the imagery of oratory, 'the best feature is always its reality and truth' (XV, 8). But the exaggerations of the imagination and of poetry also satisfy ultimately the demands of truth: 'Are we not, then, to hold that composition (being a

4

harmony of that language which is implanted by nature in man and which appeals not to the hearing only but to the soul itself), since it calls forth manifold shapes of words, thoughts, deeds, beauty, melody, all of them born at our birth and growing with our growth, and since by the means of the blending and variation of its own tones it seeks to introduce into the minds of those who are present the emotion which affects the speaker and since it always brings the audience to share in it and by the building of phrase upon phrase raises a sublime and harmonious structure: are we not, I say, to hold that harmony by these selfsame means allures us and invariably disposes us to stateliness and dignity and elevation and every emotion which it contains within itself, gaining absolute mastery over our minds?' (XXXIX, 3).

The comprehension and the work that results possess the very quality of life itself: 'The choice of proper and striking words ... is the direct agency which ensures the presence in writings, as upon the fairest statues, of the perfection of grandeur, beauty, mellowness, dignity, force, power, and any other high qualities there may be, and breathes into dead things a kind of living voice' (XXX, 1). But this happens only when we despise the love of pleasure, which debases, and the love of wealth, which corrupts. If men give in to these, the readers of poetry and the poets, too, 'will no longer lift up their eyes or have any further regard for fame, but the ruin of such lives will gradually reach its complete consummation and sublimities of soul fade and wither away and become contemptible, when men are lost in admiration of their own mortal parts and omit to exalt that which is immortal' (XLIV, 8).

Sometimes Longinus hardly seems like a Greek, and what he says of sublimity, all that about transport and the divine, misses what we most value in many of the best works of antiquity—the Venus de Milo, the Parthenon, Homer and even Sappho—some quietness or stillness, some easiness in their greatness. We see in him something that is perhaps not feverish but is close to it, an intensity greater even than that of the Stoic pantheism, close to that of some of the cults Plotinus is said to have drawn on, an intensity that later will be taken to be the mark of those who are hostile to classicism.

The thought is profound and clear, the discriminations are just, the taste superb, but the impetus is almost overrich. As, almost paradoxically, it is not in Plotinus. There, for all our reluctance to follow his transcendentalism, we see what we miss in Longinus, thought carried to greater lengths and with more interesting results, and in the very matter that is central to Longinus, leading into greater vistas.

I think Longinus has put the right things together and in the right order. His instincts and his character are sound, we might say. But however much he insists on the supremacy of thought, there remains the sense that he cherishes ecstasy at the expense of the serenity that many believe to be the sign of the mind's greatest success. The reason for this becomes clear, I think, when we examine the way he regards Nature and the poet's relation to it.

Longinus returns again and again to the idea of Nature as the formative power of men's souls and imaginings and speech. It is Nature that has appointed us to be the spectators of the whole universe and has implanted in us aspiration for the divine (XXXV, 2). Nature implants harmony in us, and language and its harmony, bringing to bear in the process of our life every variety of beauty and thought and song, and leading our life finally into a grand, comprehensive structure (XXXIX, 3). The imagination itself gives birth to speech (XV, 1).

The ideas, the analogies, return again and again to this, that man is a part of Nature, informed with its life and order and its instinctive movements towards the divine. His art, the way he selects words and manipulates figures and sounds, takes its being from this innate sense and harmony.

He implies, however, that man, in his consciousness at least, is separate from Nature, he is not immersed in it, he remains something else than the force he obeys and the divinity he praises. When we are taken up into the presence of the gods, we are not lost in the cosmic life, we remain ourselves, seeing and judging, discerning the purpose of our birth (XXXV, 3) and in the declaration that words are the very light of thought (XXX, 1) there remains the idea of the one who thinks, who is apart from what he sees.[1] And the poet, in full inspiration, lends

---

[1] This idea of the continuing self-consciousness of the inspired or ecstatic soul conforms to one of the most significant distinctions in Plotinus's reasoning about the

the stamp of his own personality even in the creation of the sublime: '[Homer] is wont himself to enter into the sublime actions of his heroes ... In truth, Homer in these cases shares the full inspiration of the combat, and it is neither more nor less than true of the poet himself that

> Mad rageth he as Arês the shaker of spears, or as mad
> flames leap
> Wild-wasting from hill unto hill in the folds of a
> forest deep,
> And the foam-froth fringeth his lips.'[1]

Sometimes Longinus seems to believe that the forces of Nature and of inspiration are the same, and we think he may be about to say that Nature is speaking through the poet. When he refers in various terms to an ecstatic experience allied to poetry,[2] we look to him to identify the divine fury Plato speaks of with this Nature that he says is working in the soul of the poet. Yet he never goes that far and instead he seems to be leading us rather differently, to some idea in which the source of ecstasy, the inspiration, is either thought or the object of thought. I think he comes close to defining beyond misinterpretation his central position when he speaks of the inspiration a poet receives from the writings of others. His expression is that many are carried away by the breath of another, 'as if inspired', and though we must necessarily think that he is here using the terms

---

[1] *Iliad*, XV, 605–7; Longinus; IX, 10–11.
[2] Terms and phrases like 'enthusiastic', (VIII, 1); and 'in a sudden moment of inspiration, as if possessed by a divine afflatus' (XVI, 2).

---

nature of contemplation, involving the ontological distinction between ἕν and νοῦς. The separation of the knower and the thing known is transcended only when there is achieved the final, perfect knowledge of the source of being. Longinus apparently never considers that possibility.

Professor P. O. Kristeller has observed that in Renaissance Neo-Platonism, and more particularly in Ficino, the self-consciousness of the inspired soul is not maintained according to the same distinctions as in Plotinus, that indeed the soul in contemplation rather easily loses the sense of its separate identity, but again in a way differently than Plotinus would have considered possible or desirable: all is absorbed in subjectivity (*Il Pensiero Filosofico di Marsilio Ficino* [Florence, 1953], p. 244).

The position of Longinus, between Plotinus and that of the later Neo-Platonists, may avoid the extremes of subjectivism and mysticism, and it may possibly rest on a common-sense analysis supported by the minimum of metaphysical commitments. One difficulty appears, however: the relationship between inspiration and truth remains in doubt.

figuratively, he compares this state with that of the oracle at Delphi: 'For many men are carried away by the spirit of others as if inspired, just as it is related of the Pythian priestess when she approaches the tripod, where there is a rift in the ground which (they say) exhales divine vapour. By heavenly power thus communicated she is impregnated and straightway delivers oracles in virtue of the afflatus. Similarly from the great natures of the men of old there are borne in upon the souls of those who emulate them (as from sacred caves) what we may describe as *effluences*, so that even those who seem little likely to be possessed are thereby inspired and succumb to the spell of the others' greatness' (XIII, 2).[1]

As much as the 'just as' and 'as if' will let him, he discusses 'inspiration' as a state deriving from both physical and spiritual causes. It would have been possible for him to combine such notions with the idea of a persuasive rationality in the source of the poet's inspiration, in the universe itself, yet he nowhere supports his analysis by ideas that were at hand to him (whether his treatise comes from the first or the third century), that the divine breath, the *pneuma*, the soul of the universe, uses the poet, or the poem he is reading, as its vessel.[2] He does not define the impetus, or what it leads to—this Nature he is so proud to depend on—as the rational and life-giving God, or the One, or the All. He may seem to speak of an invasion of the soul as the action of 'effluences' but all he is really saying is that what moves the poet, and the oracle, is divine and admirable, it is a force that comes upon him from outside himself: the excitement, the frenzy, the spell, are the accompaniment rather than the cause of the inspiration.

[1] Longinus is evidently referring to an explanation of the operation of the earth vapours upon the body of the priestess that is also repeated by Strabo, Origen, and Crysostom, among others. The vapours, or, in some interpretations, the prophetic (and fluid) soul of the universe, entered the priestess through the sexual organs. This is one way of accounting for the use of terms like *impregnation* and *fecondation* as synonyms for *inspiration*.

Gérard Verbeke gives a rather full survey of ancient thinking on this matter (*L'Evolution de la Doctrine du Pneuma* [Paris, 1945], pp. 269–70).

[2] Ideas like this are to be found in the fragments of Heracleitus, and were elaborately developed by Democritus (see Armand Delatte, *Les Conceptions de l'Enthousiasme chez les Philosophes Présocratiques* [Paris, 1934], pp. 10 and 37 in particular). Something like a compendium of theories of inspiration may be observed in Plutarch (see G. Verbeke, *L'Evolution de la Doctrine du Pneuma*, pp. 260–86).

Plutarch mentioned the theory that excitement alone, the heating of the soul, created the powerful and efficient images of the poet, and in this light the poem might be regarded as the work, not of the god, but of the man himself.[1] This view of things may help clarify Longinus's position. Longinus would agree with the main point of such a theory, that the poet is in his own character uniquely responsible for his work, yet he clearly would not agree that inspiration is a purely subjective or physiological excitement. He is too profoundly committed to the importance he places upon rationality and judgment, and he maintains unequivocally that the experience the most sublime poet communicates is a contemplative experience and not simply frenzy—we become 'spectators of the mighty whole ... [and] not even the entire universe suffices for the thought and contemplation within the reach of the human mind' (XXXV, 2–3). This is something other than frenzy, this is the achievement anticipated in the *Epinomis*, 'the desire to learn to the depth whatever is within reach of mortals, with the thought that by such means one will come to lead the best and happiest life, and after death arrive in those realms destined for those who follow virtue'.[2] As with this element in the Platonic teaching Longinus's concern with the divine is focused more on the idea of truth and nobility than on the experience of ecstasy. The elevated mind in its inspired state perceives the vastness of truth. It is for just this reason that Longinus praises Moses, 'the legislator of the Jews, no ordinary man, having formed and expressed a worthy conception of the might of the Godhead' (IX, 9). It is because Moses possesses a valid conception that he is sublime, having uttered what is indeed the appropriate embodiment of the fact, 'Let there be light'.

In one of his most elaborate expositions Longinus speaks of an instance in which argument itself attains a sublime intensity, and one is obliged, therefore, to believe that Demosthenes is kindled by the truth as much as by 'the god': 'When ... as though suddenly inspired by heaven and as it were frenzied by the God of Prophecy [Demosthenes] utters his famous oath by the champions of Greece ("assuredly ye did no wrong; I swear it by those who at Marathon stood in the forefront of the

---

[1] *De defectu oraculorum*, XL, 432–3.
[2] 986c–d.

9

danger"), in the public view by this one figure of Adjuration, which I here term *Apostrophe*, he deifies his ancestors. He brings home the thought that we ought to swear by those who have thus nobly died as we swear by Gods, and he fills the mind of the judges with the high spirit of those who there bore the brunt of the danger, and he has transformed the natural course of the argument into transcendent sublimity and passion and that secure belief which rests upon strange and prodigious oaths' (XVI, 2).

He says something very like this when he returns to the notion of elevating oneself through the work of others: 'It is well that we ourselves, also, when elaborating anything which requires lofty expression and elevated conception, should shape some idea in our minds as to how perchance Homer would have said this very thing, or how it would have been raised to the sublime by Plato or Demosthenes or by the historian Thucydides' (XIV, 1). As much as he can condense the doctrine into a few words he does so in the tremendous claim that 'sublimity raises men near the mighty mind of God' (XXXVI, 1); and at one place at least he comes close to saying that ideas in themselves possess a separate and divine existence: 'Hence also a bare idea, by itself and without a spoken word, sometimes excites admiration just because of the greatness of soul implied. Thus'—he is thinking of Homer—'the silence of Ajax in the Underworld is great and more sublime than words' (IX, 2).

It would seem, then, that whatever he means by saying that Nature has implanted in us the love of the divine, and that the gods and truth raise us as it were into their sight, the poet lives in two worlds, not one. Man, for Longinus, so magnificently the creature of Nature, is also very much what he was for the Hermetic philosophers—'he shares in the divine principle of mind or reason not merely as the lower animals and the rest of the cosmos do by being rationally ordered, but by being in some sort identified with the divine Mind';[1] and if he does not present us with an idea of an articulated hierarchy in which man has his place, he nevertheless has a view of him which by the very insistence on the capacity of man for elevation resembles the conception so important to Renaissance humanists, that man is 'at the world's centre ... [with] the power, out of the soul's

[1] C. H. Dodd, *The Interpretation of the Fourth Gospel* (Cambridge, 1953), p. 27.

judgment, to be reborn into the higher forms, which are divine'.[1]

It seems certain that either a Platonic or a mystical affirmation is supporting this 'sober intoxication'.[2] W. H. Fyfe translated Longinus's 'even in the midst of a Bacchic frenzy it is necessary to be sober' (XVI, 4) with Hamlet's advice to the players: 'in the very torrent, tempest, and, as I may say, the whirlwind of passion, you must acquire and beget a temperance that may give it smoothness'. Underlying such constancy and strength, in Longinus at least, is the firm conviction that he is treating with absolute truth, 'that secure belief which rests upon strange and prodigious oaths' (XVI, 2).

Despite the use of words like 'effluences' and 'afflatus' and 'divine breath' Longinus refrained from placing them in the context of the materialist theories of inspiration to which they properly belong.[3] The drift of his thought as well as his reticences consistently approach Platonic philosophizing,[4] although here, too, his manner is that of a critic and not a philosopher. But he makes at least one statement that points toward a psychology of the imagination that must involve a commitment because it is evidently part of an argument against one of the current doctrines of imitation, opposing those who declare that the images of the mind are merely the representations of external objects: 'In a general way the name of *image* or *imagination* is applied to every idea of the mind, in whatever form it presents itself, which gives birth to speech' (XV, 1). The significant words here are ἐννόημα which means notion or concept, or even the object of thought,[5] and γεννητικόν, which derives

[1] Pico della Mirandola, 'On the Dignity of Man', translated by E. L. Forbes, in *The Renaissance Philosophy of Man*, ed. E. Cassirer *et al.* (Chicago, 1948), p. 225.

[2] The editors refer Longinus's phrase to an illuminating passage in the *Bacchae*, 317, where the reference is to the virtue of *sophrosyne*. This word, for which temperance is a reasonably good equivalent, comes to be, I believe, the virtue of central importance to Plato's ethics and as such would have played an important part in Longinus's insistence on the necessity of nobility of character in the poet. Something of this is to be seen in Helen F. North's 'The Concept of *Sophrosyne* in Greek Literary Criticism', *Classical Philology*, XLIII (1948), 1–17.

[3] See Delatte, *Les Conceptions de l'Enthousiasme chez les Philosophes Présocratiques, passim.*

[4] It has been reckoned that Longinus refers to works of Plato nineteen times, most often to the *Timaeus*, and several times to the *Laws*.

[5] Aristotle, *Metaphysics*, 981a6; Zeno, *Stoicorum Veterum Fragmenta*, I, 19, lines 22 and 28.

from the word for engender. There is an obvious similarity here to the Stoic idea that the imagination is intermediary between the action of Nature upon the soul and the practice of thought.[1] What may be equally Stoic is the underlying supposition of the rationality of the inspiring influence, whether this is regarded as the soul of the universe or as something else. But one must at the same time keep in mind two points that Longinus stresses that would modify and perhaps transform his obligations to the Stoics—his insistence on the personal stamp each poet gives to his own, even inspired work, and what seems to be signified by his way of speaking of the way in which the imagination 'gives birth' to speech.

Posidonius appears to have been the first to argue for the existence of a creative power in each soul. Even while modifying the Stoic notion of the *anima mundi* as the source and substance of inspiration by substituting the term *idea* for *soul*, he provided for the creative power of the individual in transforming the material of his imagination.[2] In its turn this development seems to have prepared the way for Longinus's conception of the relation of the poetic achievement to the character of the poet.

As for the effect of the poet's character upon what he creates, Longinus has much to say. His treatise ends with the condemnation of the faults of the modern age, and from this we learn what makes the virtuous man. He resists selfishness, vanity, and luxuriousness, faults which breed tyranny, violence, lawlessness, and shamelessness. These destroy the qualities of greatness in the soul, and lead men to 'admire what is mortal in them, and to neglect the growth of the immortal' (XLIV, 8). The conception of virtue he stresses here, apparently as the very culmination of his work, and the plea for a return to the virtues of the republican aristocrat as well as of the philosopher, take up the note he began with in praising Nature, who has brought us into the world, for no ignoble end, but in order to share, through our understanding, in the magnificence of all things—

[1] Diogenes Laertius, VII, 45, 49 and 52; Plutarch, *De placitis philosophorum*, IV, xi.

M. W. Bundy opposes the claim of an exclusive Stoic influence upon Longinus in these matters by offering evidence of similar ideas and language in the writings of the Epicureans (*The Theory of Imagination in Classical and Mediaeval Thought* [Urbana, 1927], pp. 110–11).

[2] See Verbeke, *L'Evolution de la Doctrine du Pneuma*, p. 135.

the ecstasy of the most elevated art being at once the witness of the excellence of our birth and the proof of our capacity to share in the divine.

But it is not only the virtue with which we are endowed that qualifies us for the achievement and the vision, it is also what we ourselves cherish and follow. It is this insistence upon our own cultivation and discipline that justifies Augusto Rostagni, I believe, when he deduces from the treatise an aesthetics of creativity: 'Under the impulse of passion images are born, and also poetical expressions. In this way Longinus explains the phenomenon of art, which is form [Posidonius' *idea*], form that is alive, rooted in the depth of the spiritual nature, brought into being and motion by the inner motions of the soul ... For Longinus imitation and inspiration are a kind of *instauratio ab imis* of the inner I, a cultivation of those intellectual and moral values, of feeling and strength and character that constitute the integrity of the human being, out of which grows the sublime flower of art.'[1]

Rostagni's language carries overtones of an aestheticism that belongs more to the present century than to the early Christian period, but his fundamental conclusion seems to me to be right. Longinus does mean that the poet as an individual is contributing out of his own power and will and life what is as necessary to his achievement as any other truth.

But as I see it, the crucial question for Longinus is not the *process* of engendering, but rather what it is that enables the poet to carry on his life in his expression. It would be easy for Longinus to argue that it was reason, present in the universe as in the poet's own mind, that would manifest itself in his work, reason understood as the life force and the principle of the good life. And this would be the easier in that it would also accord with the Platonic doctrine that thought and expression are intrinsically the same,[2] although this seems to me to be something other than the extreme subjectivism Rostagni describes. Longinus is always mindful of a transcendent reality that is something other than his inner being, or even than Nature,

[1] *Scritti Minori* (Turin, 1955), I, 502 and 504 ('Superamento della retorica nell' anonimo del "Sublime" ').

[2] 'Well, then, thought and speech are the same; only the former, which is a silent inner conversation of the soul with itself, has been given the special name of thought.' *Sophist*, 263E.

13

something clearly pointed to in the famous statement that 'beautiful words are the very light of thought' (XXX, 2).

I would like to be able to argue that when Longinus says this he is speaking of words as light, in the way in which philosophy often spoke of light, as the vehicle of the soul:[1] the radiant substance by which the thing itself is known to us —whether that be a conception or an idea or the soul of the world. And what would be true of words would be true also of the images that engendered them. There was a great deal of speculation to this effect that would have been available to him, and indeed his own writing is supposed to have been the source for similar ideas in the Renaissance. But he does not in fact give us enough from which to derive a true argument.[2] The most one can do, I

[1] Quintino Cataudella has argued that Longinus's phrase is without philosophical implications and signifies only that beautiful words are the ornaments of thought ('Intorno al περι υψους, Il problema storico e il problema estetico', *Revue des Études Grecques*, XLIII [1930], 164). He points to similar phrases in Latin writers, for example: in Cicero, 'As light is to those who see, the word is to those who hear' (*De recta audiendi ratione*, V, 39E) and 'No meaning is made clear except by the light of words' (*De oratore*, III, 5, 24); and in Quintilian the remarkable parallel, 'words correspond to things, and they are perceived by their own light' (*Institutio oratoria*, VIII, Preface, par. 21).

The meaning of the phrase then becomes simply that thought and diction often explain each other, and this in turn derives from the idea probably first expressed by Philodemus, a pupil of Zeno's, that the form of expression in the arts cannot be separated from the content. (This development is rather fully discussed in Rostagni's 'Risonanze dell' Estetica di Filodemo in Cicerone', in *Scritti Minori*, I, 379–81).

If the doctrine of Philodemus is the appropriate one to refer to, then I should think it all the more necessary to grant Longinus's phrase philosophic meaning, for 'content' in Longinus with its invariable Platonic reference logically must include the idea of 'form' as well.

The fragment of Philodemus may be found in *Philodemos Über die Gedichte, Fünftes Buch*, ed. Christian Jensen (Berlin, 1923), p. 147.

[2] The critical matter has to do with theories that treat the imagination as a cognitive power, and in a certain respect the issues may be thought to derive from Aristotle's criticism of Plato in *De anima*, III, 3, where he discusses the relation of images to sense impressions. In one tradition that develops the issues raised in this controversy, the imagination comes to be spoken of as the vehicle or vestment of the soul in the same way that the soul was said to be clothed with the fifth element, or some other radiant substance. (The primary study of these matters is R. C. Kissling's 'The OXNMA-ΠNEYMA of the Neo-Platonists and the *De Insomniis* of Synesius of Cyrene', *American Journal of Philology*, XLIII (1922), 318–30). The sixth-century commentary of Simplicius on the *De anima* provides extensive comments on this notion, but in the fourth century one also may see, in Synesius, the idea that thought is embodied in the imagination, and that imagination is this very soul-matter that gods and demons and dreams inhabit (*De Insomniis*, 1292–3). Kissling points out that this conception is identical with Augustine's idea of the *anima*

believe, is to draw inferences that the statements seem to warrant and to support them by reference to the Platonism that is so generally characteristic of his thought. The only argument that can be proposed with hope of proof is the negative one—that Longinus is not defending any of the conventional doctrines of mimesis.

Such, I think, is the context in which Longinus presents us with the material of criticism, with observations and advice on figures of speech and thought, on the use of poetry for contemplation and the formation of character. And as we estimate the value of his way of thinking, this Platonic, half-mystic claim for the elevation of mind we associate with the passionate and powerful writing he calls to our minds, we are led to ask

---

spiritualis: 'the intellectual part of the soul apprehends the truth of intelligibilities abstracted from all bodily forms, and the spiritual apprehends all from corporal objects' (*De Civitate Dei*, X, c. ix, par. 2).

This same idea of the vehicle of the soul becomes the means of explaining inspiration in Porphyry: in him the prophetic pneuma, which comes from the divine power, 'enters into man and speaks through his mouth, using his soul as its "basis" '. (See E. R. Dodds, ed., *Proclus, The Elements of Theology* [Oxford, 1933], p. 314).

Philo Judaeus, who is sometimes thought to have been known to the author of *On the Sublime*, illustrates quite clearly how this idea of the vehicle of spiritual knowledge, or indeed of any knowledge, might be identified with the sense of light. He speaks of the inspiration of Moses as 'a certain impression and character of divine power which divine Moses calls by an appropriate name image'. H. A. Wolfson shows that Philo uses as synonyms for *image, impression* and *ray of light*, and goes on to explain that the basis of Philo's reasoning here is that 'the essence of the mind [is] an incorporeal image of the idea of mind' (*Philo* [Cambridge, 1947–53], I, 395). The references to Philo are *Legum Allegoria*, III, 161; *De Somniis*, I, 34; and *Quod deterius potiori insidiari soleat*, 83. Philo also speaks of the imagination as the vestment of the reason (*Leg. Alleg.*, III, 15).

The idea of light as the nature and source of truth is of course central to Platonic as well as to a number of intellectual and religious systems, and the idea of the light of the mind is indispensable to the notion of 'the inner eye'. It may very well be that this is no metaphor, as Gabriel Marcel insists (*Man against Inhumanity* [London, 1952], pp. 196–7), but if Longinus meant it merely as a metaphor this would still not extricate the statement from the Platonism that pervades the treatise. Taken philosophically the statement would agree, too, with the almost mystical intensity he ascribes to the experience of sublimity.

Robert Klein has recently suggested that the phrase in Longinus that speaks of the imagination engendering words (XV, 1) is also related to the idea of the celestial vehicle, and he goes on further to state that Longinus by his way of putting it is one of the precursors of some of the most significant theories of the Renaissance on the nature of images and symbols ('L'imagination comme vêtement de l'âme chez Marsile Ficin et Giordano Bruno', *Revue de Métaphysique et de Morale*, LXI [1956], 35n.).

one further question: is it really poetry he is talking about, is it really beautiful words and affective speech, or is it something transcendental for which poetry is only the stepping stone? Does he, in short, value enough the material of the artist, the objects of the senses, the words as sound and music and meaning? Is this the mystique of intensity, or, as he calls it, ecstasy, however sober?

For my part, I must return to one of the beginning points of this study—whatever it is that Longinus praises and worships, however pure and clear his reasoning, the vistas he opens for us are not those of an earlier Greece—there is nothing here of the Venus de Milo, or the Parthenon, or Archilochus:

ἔχουσα θαλλὸν μυρσίνης ἐτέρπετο
ῥοδῆς τε καλὸν ἄνθος, ἡ δὲ οἱ κόμη
ὤμους κατεσκίαζε καὶ μετάφρενα.

(Fr. 40)

She delights in holding a myrtle branch and the flower of a rose and her hair casts a shadow across her neck and shoulders.

—nothing of the sacred Homeric epithets, the sacrosanct formulas so clear and simple and noble—the wine-dark sea, white-handed Hera, wily Odysseus—that are above all else the things they name, by the clearest light—but not the light of the mind of God, not even the light of reason; the light in the air itself, of the Cyclades, or over Attica or Ionia. And that wonderful poem of Sappho's he has preserved for us in the name of the sublime may be thought to be the greater for not being 'divine', for being merely a recital of the facts, facts as known to mortals, to mortal eyes.

In a sense he errs by stressing the divine as he does, not that it is wrong to speak of inspiration and all that follows as being of the gods, but in being trapped as Platonists always are by knowing no way of taking the material world seriously enough. Like Plotinus and like Plato, he may be thought to solve it all by postulating hypostases and emanations—and he has no word for incarnation.

And here again Longinus's reticence in philosophizing is his strength. By not being explicit in these matters he avoids the critic's greatest danger, conceiving of the work of art as having

16

an existence apart from what brought it into being. Leaving so much to inference, he gives us enough latitude, so that we are free to regard even the sublime and the work that brings us to that state in ways that stop short of a particular commitment to the philosophy of the absolute. This is his wonderful tact, persuading us of the rightness of his judgment and of the supremacy of ecstasy such as he describes, all the while holding us true to our integral humanity and its reason, and leaving us free to keep poetry separate from philosophy and from religion.

In later centuries poets and critics will share his estimate of the importance of the elevation of the spirit words are capable of, and for many reasons other philosophic and religious issues will become involved. The problems of Dante and Michelangelo and Milton are also the problems of sublimity and they may be even more complex. But because he is apart from Christianity and something of the merely *honnête homme* he must continue to serve us as the point of repair for every effort to estimate the nature of the highest achievements of poetry.

DANTE

AT SOME POINT in the *Paradiso*, perhaps very early, perhaps as late as the appearance of Bernard, the writing attains a splendour that thereafter never lessens. The subject of the poetry now is what it means to be in the presence of God. The experience is the kind Saint Paul spoke of and that Dante himself described in the letter to Can Grande—'the intellect is so engulfed in the thing for which it longs, which is God, that memory cannot follow'.

Mysticism endangers any decent human balance, and the relation of a vision as by one who was himself caught up into the heavens could have disintegrated into evident nonsense or unfeeling rationality. And instead, there is only success, power and clarity and dignity.

The effect goes beyond anything Longinus could have pointed to when he made his claim that sublime poetry allows us to believe that for the moment we share the power of the gods. None of those he spoke of, not even that Nature that was his oracle, was the creator of a universe. And although Longinus may have believed in a world soul, pervading the lives of gods as well as mortals, the ecstatic apprehension of the truth could not be the same as it was for Dante, to be defined by the idea of the mystical union of the soul with the omnipotent creator. If Dante succeeds, as he is thought to, in communicating something like the sense of reality and of truth in the last book, the achievement is poetry of a deeper intensity within a narrower vista than Longinus had in mind.

What is so obviously the subject of the *Paradiso* is also a necessary part of the conception of the rest of the *Divine Comedy*. In the story of Ulysses in the *Inferno* the verse moves with a power that seems to express the fullest capacities of human understanding and expression:

> 'Tutte le stelle già de l' altro polo
>   vedea la notte, e 'l nostro tanto basso,
>   che non surgea fuor del marin suolo.
> Cinque volte racceso e tante casso
>   lo lume era di sotto da la luna,
>   poi che 'ntrati eravam ne l' alto passo,
> quando n' apparve una montagna, bruna
>   per la distanza, e parvemi alta tanto
>   quanto veduta non avea alcuna.
> Noi ci allegrammo, e tosto tornò in pianto;
>   chè de la nova terra un turbo nacque,
>   e percosse del legno il primo canto.
> Tre volte if fè girar con tutte l' acque;
>   a la quarta levar la poppa in suso
>   e la prora ire in giù, com' altrui piacque,
> infin che 'l mar fu sopra noi richiuso.'
>
>   (*Inferno*, XXVI, 127–42)

'Night already saw the other pole, with all its stars; and ours so low, that it rose not from the ocean floor.

Five times the light beneath the Moon had been re-kindled and quenched as oft, since we had entered on the arduous passage,

when there appeared to us a Mountain, dim with distance; and to me it seemed the highest I had ever seen.

We joyed, and soon our joy was turned to grief: for a tempest rose from the new land, and struck the forepart of our ship.

Three times it made her whirl round with all the waters; at the fourth, made the poop rise up and prow go down, as pleased Another, till the sea was closed above us.'

And it is not only in scenes where the thought is sustained by the most serious conceptions that we recognize their unity with the culmination of the work. There are many places where the ideas are the simplest, the most earth-bound and ordinary, in similes or fragments of an action, in which the power and the magnitude of the whole poem come alive with the light of the *Paradiso* itself:

> Quali i fioretti, dal notturno gelo
>   chinati e chiusi, poi che 'l sol li 'mbianca
>   si drizzan tutti aperti in loro stelo,
> tal me fec' io di mia virtute stanca,
>   e tanto buono ardire al cor mi corse,
>   ch' i' cominciai come persona franca:
> 'Oh pietosa colei che mi soccorse!'
>
> (Inferno, II, 127–33)

As flowerets, by the nightly chillness bended down and closed, erect themselves all open on their stems when the sun whitens them:
    thus I did, with my fainting courage; and so much good daring ran into my heart, that I began as one set free:
'O compassionate she, who succoured me!'

At times there are even single phrases that seem to embody the most elevated understanding. Such, I think, is *il lago del cor*, 'the lake of the heart', concentrating a degree of passion and thought one would hardly think that words could bear, and that indeed seems to have a life of its own:

> Allor fu la paura un poco queta
>   che nel lago del cor m' era durata
>   la notte ch' io passai con tanta pieta.
>
> (Inferno, I, 19–21)

Then the fear was somewhat calmed, which had continued in the lake of my heart the night that I passed so piteously.

It seems that in a certain sense Dante is everywhere the same. He writes of all that he has seen in the world and it is always to the same end. He may be presenting us with some sight of the hideous or the trivial, and his hate and his scorn are as grand as his praise. Whenever, after an interval, one returns to almost any passage, what at first might have seemed merely life-sized, has become larger, every word has greater stature, every image takes on heroic size. And all the while one continues to remember the smallness of the central figure, this lost man dependent on a guide come from the dead, this human being who is not only the central person but the teller of the story. Every word is his, in its passion and in its plaintiveness, the deprecation of the human belongs with the heroic—

Ah quanto a dir qual era è cosa dura—
(Inferno, I, 4)

Ah! how hard it is to tell what it was like—

the pathetic and the ironic magnify the pride and greatness.

Such a mingling of the great and small intensifies the grandeur and complexity of his conception, and every accent, every intonation, witnesses the magnificence of a mind in control of its deepest and most comprehensive efforts. The trivial asserts the fullness of the command of the great, everything is contained within one focus, every detail, even the smallest, displays the confidence of thought that has arrived at its end. And the reader is immediately and for ever at ease, the verse, the progression of the narrative, the diversions, the reminiscences, the humour, never take him away from the main thing, the integrity of the vision, of its complexity and insight, of the mind that has satisfied itself. The familiarity of the details of every day only confirms the grandeur of the thought and of the poem.

What is involved in such a technique is more than a trick of rhetoric or poetic. It depends on what the poet started with, an idea of the glories of Paradise that was to lead him to relate the story of a man who has become confused, the chances of Hell suddenly clear to him, and his weakness always on the point of overthrowing him. It is because every idea and every word he chooses is pervaded with his sense of the final glory that the most particular details of the journey, the most apparently trivial ones, like the triviality of the man himself, and the triviality of flowers, of hoar frost, of a peasant slapping his thigh in disappointment, reveal the power of the whole vision.

E come stella in cielo il ver si vide—
(Paradiso, **XXVIII**, 87)

And like a star in heaven the truth is seen—

a point of light in the sky, a celestial body, becomes a way of seeing what is never seen, but of knowing it as if one did see it, the truth of existence itself. The comprehension is both grand and intimate.

The integrity that Dante stamps on every syllable of the poem has led its readers to propose various definitions for what

Longinus would call the conception of the work, to suggest some one thing, whether an idea or an image, that could be thought of as the seed of the whole work. Such suggestions can be richly useful in reasoning about the quality of the poetry, and particularly its greatness.

Edoardo Coli thought that the originating impetus of the poem was something he preferred to call an image rather than an idea or a system of ideas. As he spoke of it, Dante was guided throughout the work by an image that was always before him of the very scene of the Earthly Paradise. This was the theatre in which Beatrice was to appear, and it was also the world out of which she was born—'the cool, morning freshness, the limpid, fragrant air, the pure sky'.[1]

There are other 'seeds' one could speak of similarly as the original impetus, with as much and as little conclusiveness as this, that would point to something surely constant in Dante's conception as the work progressed, the idea of a pilgrimage into the light, the idea of a person seen in a dream, all kinds of visual or visionary appearances that bear the burden of complex significances. But the idea of the Earthly Paradise as the originating conception has a particular appeal because it brings together so many things that were part of the intrinsic teaching of the poem as well as what belongs to the sense of actuality; it continuously maintains the sense of light and the clearly visible, of immediacy and joy, of the imminence of fulfilment, of human existence at its purest.

Everything in the poem would follow from this initial image, the voyager would be seen at the very beginning not only against the light of Hell but in the light of the remembrance of that Spring-like vision of Paradise, and the means of the restoration of the full light of that vision would control the progress of the journey and of the poem.

Another effort, perhaps a more remarkable one, to demonstrate that 'the unity of the poem presupposes a dominating idea that runs right through it and pervades it from start to finish' is Egidio Gorra's argument that Dante's idea of the significance of his meeting with Beatrice, which he first began to measure in the time of the *Vita Nuova*, ultimately became the revelation of all that life could hold for him.

[1] *Il Paradiso Terrestre Dantesco* (Florence, 1897), pp. 217–18.

Gorra argued against Coli by proposing that the genesis of the poem lay partly in the experiences related in the *Vita Nuova* and partly in the difficulties of his life in politics and in exile. The essential point of his argument is that the great work is the summation of a life. The idea of Eden was not the original conception of the work, but a subsequent one, when the mind of the poet, tired from exile, felt the need to rid himself of the affairs of the earth in order to attain a more serene existence. It was under such circumstances that he conceived of the Earthly Paradise and the Celestial, returning to what had occupied his mind in the composition of the *Vita Nuova* as primarily the remembrance of a vision. The idea of the *Inferno*, of descending like Aeneas into the lower regions, came after his exile, when, following the ecstasies of youth, there succeeded the tempests of his mature life. He would never have conceived of Beatrice sending a guide to lead him through the lower world unless that world itself, the world of society and politics, had been the initial impetus towards his thinking of the need for salvation. 'The political idea was united with the religious, a single conception in which the moral, the religious and the political elements formed an indivisible and organic unity. At that point Dante's thought and feeling had reached maturity, and he girded himself to make the poem. The spirit of Dante, that in its youthful boldness made a pilgrimage of the flesh and pushed itself into the very heavens in order to be drunk with an endless happiness, was called back by the uproar of the affairs of the world where it tasted the unspeakable griefs that the world creates for men, and then he went forth again to contemplate the place of eternal peace.'[1]

This point of view is particularly attractive since it depends on the idea that the work of many years took shape out of the changes in Dante's life, and in suggesting a kind of improvisation in the conception of the *Divine Comedy* demanded by fortune itself. I do not know how this point of view can be successfully defended, but it has the certain value of not relating the poem too simply to a single idea which, as an idea, is supposed to account for the entire procedure of composing the work.

Then there is a more philosophical way of attempting to

[1] 'Per la genesi della *Divina Commedia*', in *Fra Drammi e Poemi* (Milan, 1900), pp. 181–2.

explain the unity of the poem. Umberto Cosmo, for instance, has argued that the illuminating flash that led Dante on was the idea 'that order is the informing principle of the universe ... This concept first flashed before Dante's mind in all its vastness when he was writing the fourth book of the *Convivio*. At the time he was trying to account for the workings of history. It seemed to him that history was subject to the intervention of God. It was like a world in which freedom reigned, and hence a world that followed no predictable course. The purpose of God's intervention was to bring this world back to the ways that He had predestined it to follow *ab aeterno*. It had begun on that remote day when "the most high and most indivisible divine consistory of the Trinity", with the object of "enduing humanity with new strength", had resolved to make the whole of history culminate in the birth of Christ. Jewish history and Roman history were equally divine because each prepared the way for Catholic Rome ...

'Contemplating the world of nature and history from these heights, Dante felt the airy fancies which had been vibrating in his mind ever since the day of his "wondrous vision" falling into line with this concept, blending with the new and incomparably more immense vision, and assuming an organic form. For with its harmonies, its symmetry, its rhythm—in short, with its systematic arrangement—even the poetic organism which he was creating was bound to reflect the concept to which his labours were subordinated. The journey to heaven which had as its object the glorification of Beatrice assumed the wider significance of a spiritual ascent into the presence of God. Here the poet's purpose was to discover in Him the informing principle of the universe and to inculcate into his being the rhythm of divine administration. The story of his spiritual life became the ideal of men's spiritual lives, a pattern for all to follow. The world beyond became an enormous mirror of this world because in it the justice of God finds perfect expression. The poetic aim of transporting this world into the next so that the one might take its pattern from the other became an ethical philosophy. All problems were solved in the revelation of the heavenly order, and the whole of history was influenced by the direct experience of its working. Science and history became basic elements in the organism which the poet was creating. All the notions associated with religion and politics became part and parcel of it—the necessity of the universal monarchy for the regulation of human society, the conception of the two guides charged with the task of leading the community along the path of order, the heavy responsibility of their high office. The duty of poets—of great poets—to recall them to a sense of their obligations when they erred became a vocation, akin to the mission which at certain moments in history God entrusts to some hero—namely, to compensate for the shortcomings of the guides.'[1]

All this goes back to that original desire to glorify Beatrice in his earliest work, and as there it found its expression in lyric poetry, so to the end the lyrical impetus, 'the lyrical fervour and intuition', would shape his most comprehensive thought. 'Everything springs from this intuition, and everything may be traced back to it. It is behind the poet's conception of his journey; it is behind the so-called theological romance. Even the question of science appears in a different light from that in which scholars have been too readily inclined to consider it. It is easy to regard the two cantos of the *Paradiso* that are concerned with the angels as a mere theological treatise. But if we bear in mind that the scene is the *Primum Mobile*, which communicates its essence to the whole universe, that the "movement and virtue of the holy circles" are derived from the blest movers, and that on the very threshold of the *Primum Mobile* Beatrice had indulged in a lyrical effusion in which she attributed the disorder of the world to greed, and foretold the regeneration of the world, then we see how that long discourse originated from the poet's intuition, and we can account for Beatrice's fierce attacks on bad preachers who misrepresent the word of God. The word of God is the truth that is inherent in this metaphysical concept.'[2]

This interpretation seems to me to give ideas as ideas too much precedence in the work of poetry, to the degree that it seems less sound than Coli's idea of the image of the Terrestrial Paradise. On the other hand, it gives a useful and necessary emphasis to the intellectuality of the poem.

[1] *A Handbook to Dante Studies*, translated by David Moore (Oxford, 1950), pp. 163–4.
[2] Ibid., p. 166.

One must also take serious account of whatever relates the work to the mysticism of the author. Francesco Biondolillo is one of the recent writers who has done this in a rather sustained way, and his main point is that it is precisely Dante's mysticism that controls everything. He believes that Dante conceived of art as itself a divine light, the immediate instrument of a miraculous state of mind in which the individual feels himself reaffirmed in his native inclination to the Good, and at the same time feels his humanity dissolved in light. It becomes, as art, the vision of a world all the more vast as it becomes more intense. It is in itself an increasing conquest over himself, it is itself the evidence that his moral will has become infinite and ideal, and that in his entire humanity he is sharing in the infinite. 'To be a poet is to manifest that light that is created within his spirit by the Divine Will and by virtue of which he can conquer his humanity, and to affirm his ideals was the same as to live as a human, which is to say, to actualize his ideals, to realize and make concrete the divine form impressed in his soul, form in which substance and accident and their being are joined together.'[1]

The effect of such a way of reading Dante is to regard the work as the embodiment of an inner state, of the soul in its suspension between the two poles of Evil and Good, the depths of Hell, the heights of Heaven, and to make the poem at every moment a drama of the most intense conflict between the self and the conquest of the divine.

Such a reduction of Dante's poetry either to pure mysticism or pure subjectivism confuses matters when it comes to considering the progression of the poem, and the order of the treatment of ideas. In effect, it makes everything occur at the same instant and abolishes the idea of time as part of the structure of the work. And if this is a valid criticism, it nevertheless ought not to detract from the substantial value of Biondolillo's idea, which is most valuable for the argument that the vividness of poetry is affected by something other than ideas and the power of the imagination, and that in Dante it is particularly defined by the conviction of the mystical nature of the light of his mind. Biondolillo would make the progress of the poem arbitrary, as reason judges such matters, but the order

[1] *Poetica e Poesia di Dante* (Messina, 1948), p. 20.

would be determined by the nature of a mystical vision. Each image as each event would have a visionary authority to account for the order in which it appears, and as such they would be presented to us in much the way Blake presented an account of one of his experiences:

> To my friend Butts I write
> My first vision of light,
> On the yellow sands sitting.
> The sun was emitting
> His glorious beams
> From Heaven's high streams.
> Over sea, over land,
> My eyes did expand
> Into regions of air,
> Away from all care;
> Into regions of fire,
> Remote from desire;
> The light of the morning
> Heaven's mountains adorning:
> In particles bright,
> The jewels of light
> Distinct shone and clear.

This is to say that any emphasis one accepts in accounting for the unity of the poem's conception must acknowledge that Dante's style throughout is characterized by the fundamental interest of uniting the magnificent and the intimate, and that this is as much a matter of technique as it is an element at the centre of his faith and his doctrine.

Ideas like these enrich our enjoyment of the *Divine Comedy*, but even while they are helping to increase our understanding of the work as it moves towards its marvellous conclusion we are aware that much more is holding us than the unfolding of conceptions and the articulation of thought. A picture here and there, the sight of a great body lifting its head above a tomb, a phrase—*nel lago del cor*—or the most deceptively quiet of similes—

> e come stella in cielo il ver si vide—

so conquers our attention that we suddenly forget everything we have so far learned about the poem, all its structure and theology, all we have learned to bring to bear upon this work of another age, and we are taken out of the world of ideas and understanding into mere wonder. And when we come back to the story again we recognize that here, too, Dante is exploiting a technique. He has a way of using concrete language so that it brings an image so close to us it seems we might touch it (*come stella*), and at the very moment we see it most clearly we become absorbed in something else. In the very instant he says other-wise Dante is also telling us that the truth is never seen, a star is, or an image, or whatever stands for the truth, but not the truth—he is telling us that there is another means of sight than the eyes.

And 'the lake of the heart'—so laboriously conceived in the reference to contemporary psychology—has another effect than the demonstrable meaning, the more immediate and more im-portant effect of creating the sense of depth and darkness in the treasury of the individual life. The phrase has a power no explanation touches, a power that rests in the identity of the image with what we know and love best in ourselves, some-thing neither deep nor dark nor blood.

There is present in such achievements as this what we must think of as an ultimately personal truth, not only Dante's but our own, something it seems no one but ourselves could know of, a sense of identity beyond which we never expect to inquire. And more than that, a bond is created between ourselves and the phrase that we would no more care to do without than we would care to do without thought.

Such words move us in a way one willingly compares with Longinus's description of the greatest effects of poetry, but there is also an extraordinary difference. Dante puts us in touch with what he sees as if it were nothing other than our relation-ship to truth, and the power which one may speak of as comparable to that of the immortal gods is not so much shared, which is Longinus's term, as possessed.

When we compare this way of writing with Archilochus's 'the shadow of dark hair across a shoulder', we see that the difference is a difference as if in the very medium. The light by which we see the shadow on the girl's shoulder is like the light of the sun itself, loved, so to speak, as the sun might be thought to love what it sees. This would be a power Archilochus would share with Apollo, if one might risk translating Longinus's claim that the sublime poet raises us into the very ways of the gods themselves by naming the particular gods. The same loving and yet detached clarity is in that poem of Sappho's Longinus preserved for us, 'Like a god that man seems'. What the Greeks see and tell us of they leave so to speak untouched, to its own clear existence. And what Dante does is to make everything he writes of a part of the power of life within him and within us. Where the Greek poet keeps his distance, Dante annihilates it. This is partly a matter of technique, but it has been made possible only through the acceptance of a particular philosophy, and especially a philosophy of language.

When Longinus said that words are the very light of thought, whatever context for that one would supply from Posidonius, or even from Plotinus, the emphasis would be to the effect that Greek poetry itself explains. The light of the mind is like the light of the sun, present everywhere and for everyone to use in order to see things as if they existed independently of the mind. But the images of Dante's poetry are seen differently, as it were by a light that is only within the mind. Dante's philosophy of language has indeed the special purpose of relating the light of truth to the individual experience and conscience. It is a further development of the Neo-Platonic way that was not known to Longinus, and it manifests itself not only in Dante's theory but in his very way of using words.

Dante's theories of poetry and of language appear to be coherent. His thought is elaborate and subtle and though it involves what seem to the modern reader often grotesque assumptions, it can always be translated into ideas that conform to experience.

He begins by distinguishing between the language of men before the Fall and afterwards, and to speak of what happened after the building of the Tower of Babel. He distinguishes, too, between the way in which angels converse and humans, and all this becomes the necessary preface to the cardinal affirmation: reason is the distinguishing faculty of human beings. They create bodies for their thoughts, words, which are the sensible signs of the reason that is implanted in them, and through this alliance of reason and the senses men communicate with each other.

Reason—this is the way his argument continues—is a

divine light, and it is universal, generating in everyone's mind the universal ideas that derive from the Divine Mind.[1] And while individuals differ in their expressions of ideas, and indeed in their language, communication is nevertheless possible because in each individual there exists the common rational nature which is in some sense transferred to the words with which they embody their thoughts.

'Since, then, man is not moved by natural instinct but by reason, and reason itself differs in individuals in respect of discernment, judgment, and choice, so that each one of us appears almost to rejoice in his own species, we are of opinion that no one has knowledge of another by means of his own actions or passions, as a brute beast; nor does it happen that one man can enter into another by spiritual insight, like an angel, since the human spirit is held back by the grossness and opacity of its mortal body. It was therefore necessary that the human race should have some sign, at once rational and sensible, for the intercommunication of its thoughts, because the sign, having to receive something from the reason of one and to convey it to the reason of another, had to be rational; and since nothing can be conveyed from one reason to another except through a medium of sense, it had to be sensible; for, were it only rational, it could not pass from the reason of one to that of another; and were it only sensible it would neither have been able to take from the reason of one nor to deposit in that of another.'[2]

Dante's doctrine of the relation of the conception and the utterance is Aristotelian: that words take their value from images within the mind in which is to be seen, sensible though that image is, the form of the intelligible idea.[3] And the sound of the voice that bears a meaning does so because it has received its impetus from the soul: its content corresponds, however the concept is confined by the nature of the senses and the physical nature of sound, to an image within the mind.[4]

[1] A most useful account of Dante's obligations to Aristotle and the Scholastics in this matter is supplied in an appendix to the edition of the *Convivio* of Busnelli and Vandelli (Florence, 1954), II, 392–404. Dante makes particularly significant statements in the *Convivio*, IV, xxi, 5, and the *Purgatorio*, XVIII, 55–60.

[2] *De Vulgari Eloquentia*, I, iii, translated by A. G. Ferrers Howell (Temple Classics).

[3] *De Anima*, III, 7–8 (431–2).

[4] *De Vulgari Eloquentia*, I, iii, 1–3. Bruno Nardi comments on Dante's obligation to Aristotle here in *Dante e la Cultura Medievale* (Bari, 1949), p. 236.

Manzoni thought that the *De Vulgari Eloquentia* was primarily a treatise on the language of poetry, and this may go too far but it makes the essential point. Dante is indeed saying that the curial language, which was what he called the noblest form of speech, was in fact the language of the greatest poetry. It was to be found in varying degrees in all the Italian dialects, and it found its proper form in the diction of the *canzone*. From his own reading he was able, he thought, to show that the *canzone* brought this language to perfection, and inasmuch as the *canzoni* were in the vernacular, the nobility was inherent in the speech itself.

The question then became—what is there, in a people as in a poet, that works to this marvellous achievement, that discovers and forms out of the mother speech, the words and the poetry that express the highest wisdom and beauty and truth? To that question he found the answer in a particular human faculty that he as others before him called *discretio*, discernment. This, he said, is that faculty that distinguishes things 'according to the ends to which they are ordained' (*Convivio*, I, xi, 3). This is to the reason in men as the eyes are to the sensitive soul (I, xi, 3), and it is inborn (*De Vulgari Eloquentia*, II, vii, 7).

It is a 'light' (*Convivio*, I, xi, 4) that points the way to knowledge according to the purposes of knowledge. It is the gift of God and of the Muses, and each man, as he reads the work of the greatest poets and the greatest prose writers, finds his own culture enriched, his taste refined, and his thought ennobled.[1]

It appears that Dante conceives of the creation of a most noble language for poetry as the work of many persons endowed with discernment, refining and strengthening their culture through its aid. This faculty, however subjectively thought of by an individual, is in fact diffused through the nation and the race, and in the best and noblest individuals it may be seen working towards a common end. When he reasons

[1] Professor Passerin D'Entrèves has shown that Dante extended Aquinas's idea of the function of the *lumen rationis* to the field of language — Saint Thomas related it primarily to ethics (*Dante as a Political Thinker* [Oxford, 1952], p. 91). But Dante has done more than extend the range of the faculty, particularly with respect to discernment, he has given it a more subjective character than it has with the scholastics. (See Francesco Di Capua, *Insegnamenti Retorici Medievali e Dottrine Estetiche Moderne nel* 'De Vulgari Eloquentia' *di Dante*, n. d., p. 68.)

in this way, particularly about the Italian people, Dante is extending the idea of discernment as an individual light to an idea of something like a national consciousness defined in part by the speech the nation holds in common. But there is more to it than this, as scholars have pointed out for a long time— the common *discretio* is not merely to be thought of as the spirit of law and in particular of Roman Law.[1] The inborn light of reason, *lumen rationis*, given by God and therefore gracious, *gratiosum*, imprints the law of nature and of reason in men's hearts, it inspires them with the ideal of justice, and thus informed and directed men pursue knowledge 'towards the ends to which they are ordained'. And by extension, the language their discernment helps them to is not a concrete but an ideal language, 'an abstract standard or form from which to descend to particulars and judge them ... It is ... something to be discovered and revealed, like "that panther we are in pursuit of who leaves her scent everywhere and is nowhere apparent ..."[2] "This shall be the new light, the new sun, which shall rise when the wonted sun shall set, and shall give light to them who are in darkness and in shadow as to the wonted sun, which shines not for them"' (*Convivio*, I, xiii, 12).[3]

This conception of an innate power, part judgment, part an emplastic force, implies that there is still another principle underlying the human reason, perhaps the principle of life itself that gives reason its form and validity. But however far removed the ultimate power is supposed to be, this is apparently only another way of affirming the presence of the divine within the human, another way of proposing an explanation of the means by which God manifests Himself in Nature. In this instance, it is Dante's way of expressing the traditional view of the working of inspiration. Whereas Democritus and Plato could on occasion explain the power of men to speak enthralling truth as the effect of vapours from the bowels of the earth upon

[1] See Aristide Marigo's introduction to the *De Vulgari Eloquentia* (3rd edition by Pier Giorgio Ricci, Florence, 1957), pp. lxxviii–lxxix.

[2] Passerin D'Entrèves, *Dante as a Political Thinker*, p. 94. The quotation is from the *De Vulgari Eloquentia*, I, xvi, i.

[3] Translated by P. H. Wicksteed (Temple Classics), pp. 59–60.

The significance for poetry of the idea of light in the mind has been studied by many scholars, and Professor J. A. Mazzeo has brought many of their conclusions to bear upon his criticism of the idea in Dante, especially in *Structure and Thought in the Paradiso* (Ithaca, 1958), pp. 79–83.

their bodies, Dante avoids the physiological emphasis and keeps closer to the idea that the Logos of the universe uses the reasoning capacity of man as its intermediary. Dante's 'light of reason' is part of a conception of the way in which men are understood to fulfil the purpose of their being. The idea is not much unlike Longinus's—'to be as it were spectators of the mighty universe' (XXXV, 2). And also as it is in Longinus, the full functioning of the faculty depends on the moral soundness of the poet, as Professor Passerin D'Entrèves has indicated.

What is remarkable in Dante's reasoning is that it helps account for the most characteristic feature of his own poetry, the stamp of his individuality even on the most elevated expression.

The idea that Love is the inspirer of Dante's poetry—

> 'I' mi son un, che quando
> Amor mi spira, noto, e a quel modo
> ch' e' ditta dentro vo significando.'
> (*Purgatorio*, XXIV, 52–4)

> 'I am one who, when Love inspires me take note, and go setting it forth after the fashion which he dictates within me.'

has been shown many times to be consistent with much else Dante has said of the nature of inspiration. The famous *canzone* in the *Vita Nuova, Donne ch' avete intelletto d'amore*, accords with this and provides an indication of the system of ideas that supports the doctrine. While obviously in harmony with the Platonic tradition,[1] it is supported by scholastic reasoning as well as the example of several of his fellows in the *dolce stil nuovo*. In Dante's poetry Beatrice was not only a human but an angel, and the love he declares for her is expressed as not only an adoration, but an intuition of the intellect, an elaborate intellectualizing.[2] And just as the traditional psychology affirms the spiritual union of the soul with that which it loves,[3] in the *Vita Nuova* Beatrice becomes the means, the loved object, whose nature governs the soul of Dante, not merely in

[1] Professor Mazzeo in his chapter, 'Dante and the Phaedrus Tradition of Poetic Inspiration', has written fully and clearly on this matter (*Structure and Thought in the Paradiso*, pp. 1–24).

[2] Alfredo Cesareo, 'Amor mi spira … ', in *Miscellanea di Studi Critici edita in Onore di Arturo Graf* (Bergamo, 1903), p. 539.

[3] See, for example, Aquinas, *Summa Theologica*, I-II, quaestio xxviii, a. 1 and 2.

the way of the spirit purifying the desires and liberating them from the bondage of the body, but as an angel in Heaven inducting him into the nobility and splendour of the Heavenly existence.[1]

And what is said of the power of Beatrice over his life is to be taken to apply to the power of love over his art. '*Quando Amor mi spira* signifies, that when the love of Beatrice, which is to say of the celestial Intelligence on which I am intent, burns within me, I write down according to what it expresses within me; *ed a quel modo ch'ei ditta dentro vo significando*, this means that I declare all that it causes to well up in me, thoughts of justice and truth, the sense of humility and of virtue, images of a greater than earthly beauty, and hopes of heavenly felicity.'[2]

Cesareo develops the fullest implications of the doctrine by applying to the statement the fourfold manner of interpretation that Dante himself approved: 'The literal meaning is: when Love, considered as a person, speaks within me, I write and explain point by point all that he tells me. The allegorical meaning is: when Love, considered as the adoration of intellectual beauty, stirs within me, I express the pure and noble thoughts he wakens in me. The moral meaning is: when Love, considered as the source of Good, turns towards me, I write and express the qualities of honour and humility and righteousness that he kindles in me. And the anagogical meaning is: when Love, the first cause, *Love that moves the sun and the other stars*, God, succours me with his light, I write and put down the visions of heavenly knowledge:

> pan de li angeli, del quale
> vivesi qui ma non sen vien satollo.
>
> > (*Paradiso*, II, 11–12)

bread of angels whereby life is here sustained but wherefrom none cometh away sated.[3]

The conclusion one may draw is that Dante's love for Beatrice leads his mind to the grasp of ideas which in their turn are the inspiration of his poetry. Although a mortal she becomes the image of divine beauty and a form of the Heavenly Intelligence; she forms the mind of the one who loves her, instilling virtue and knowledge and nobility. His mind is now

---

[1] Cesareo, p. 540.   [2] Ibid., p. 541.   [3] Ibid., pp. 541–2.

all-embracing, it includes a true conception of her and of himself. In beholding these two he beholds the universe, with all the variations of good and evil in Hell and Purgatory and Paradise. Love has become the impelling power and the director of his nature, it has become the means of discovering and fulfilling his truth as it has become the means of knowing hers.

Inspiration follows, then—his reasoning goes—from the love of an individual. But the principle of love is everywhere the same, it works to the same end throughout the universe, and what Dante says of Beatrice and of the God of Love he says also of the language with which he speaks of her.

From the beginning, he said, he possessed 'the most perfect love of his mother tongue' (*Convivio*, I, xii, 2). This was engendered in him by the excellence of the language itself. Again there is the doctrine that the one who loves is united with that he loves, in this matter a love defined by truth and reason and the spirit of the illustrious vernacular, 'illustrious, cardinal, courtly, and curial' (*De Vulgari Eloquentia*, I, xvii, 1). It seems that Dante is here saying that the excellence of the vernacular depends upon the beauty that is the splendour of truth, it shines within it, *illustre*, and it is indeed the beauty of the ideal that shines through sensible things.[1] And just as the first movement of his love for Beatrice is towards her as a person before he has come to know of her heavenly existence, so in poetry his first concern is with the words themselves as words.[2]

Words differ, in their very character as it were (*De Vulgari Eloquentia*, II, vii), and are accordingly fit for different purposes, but there are certain ones that serve the noblest ends, even the sublime.[3] All that is essential to language is divine, which was itself created at the time of the creation of the soul (*De Vulgari Eloquentia*, I, vi, 4), and it is by virtue of such excellence that the discernment of poets naturally makes use of it for their own most exalted purposes. For Longinus words are the light by which thought sees, but for Dante they are the embodiment of light.

---

[1] Marigo has shown how this argument is derived from Saint Thomas (*De Vulgari Eloquentia*, Introduction, pp. lxxvii–lxxviii).

[2] Marigo, p. lxxxvi. Professor Charles Singleton has developed a comprehensive theory of Dante's achievement in an interpretation of Dante's use of language as an interrelationship of the literal and the symbolic (for example, in his *Dante Studies* I [Cambridge, 1954]).

[3] Dante's word *fastigiositate* is translated by Marigo as *sublimità* (II, vii, 7).

In short, God's creation is informed by a light that works always to one end, His own praise, in the creatures of the world and in their creations—in the life and beauty of men and women and in the words that, as rational creatures, they are provided with.

It is the nature of the poet's subject that in part determines his success (*Convivio*, I, xi, 12), and as his subject seeks its proper end so does the language that expresses it, rising according to the laws of its own nature to its highest perfection (*De Vulgari Eloquentia*, I, xviii). And the vernacular that is his instrument, his and his people's, as the form that is proper to him, 'tends to realize completely its power and nobility in an ever more intimate cohesion of all its elements'.[1]

It was his native tongue, Dante said, that introduced him into the ways of knowledge and perfection (*Convivio*, I, xiii, 5). His love for it was also perfect and thus it became possible for him to exchange the word thought for soul, so thoroughly did what he love become his very self. He was even able to speak of life itself as thought, which is to say the contemplation of God: 'I say then that "the life of my heart" (that is my inner life) "was wont to be a sweet thought" ... namely, that thought which often went to the "Sire" of them to whom I speak, which is God; that is to say that I, in thought, contemplated the kingdom of the blessed' (*Convivio*, II, vii, 5).

His reasoning takes him all the way. What are presented as metaphors in the poetry of the *canzoni*, and in his own poems in the praise of love, are equally expressions of a philosophy of language that comprehends his deepest commitments: 'Dante wished to account for that impalpable world that he felt stirring within him and that he could not explain except in that vulgar speech that had now become his soul.'[2]

As I understand it, Dante's philosophizing reaches the point where it accounts for the basis of his conception of the *Divine Comedy*. If he thinks of his own inner life in its deepest experience as united with the life of the language he has now mastered, and if he believes that in this process he has come face to face with God and with all truth, he must in the poem as in the philosophizing stand outside the very expression of his union with what

---

[1] Marigo, Introduction to the *De Vulgari Eloquentia*, p. lxxii.
[2] Giulio Bertoni, 'Il "De Vulgari Eloquentia",' *Archivum Romanicum*, XX (1936), 98.

he knows and loves. He is not in truth lost in contemplation, he remains the observer and commentator on one who is. In the poem he presents himself in the frame of the universe, as one caught up in a vision, but he is also someone outside the vision, describing it as it seemed to that amazed mortal. At every point, in the philosophy as in the poem. Dante remains himself, the particular human being, Alighieri, admiring the divine vastness and reason—'va significando', the one whose pilgrimage is far from ended even as he contemplates the end. The very increase in the scope of his thought and the increase in the depth of his wisdom thus comes to seem an extension of the irony of his fundamental conception, the irony and the marvel of the union of the great and the little.

The love that unites him with what he loves, with Beatrice and with God, and with 'the words that have become his soul', continues to affirm his individuality, all that remains distinct from what he loves. The affirmation of the union is an affirmation in terms that remain his. This is the *point d'appui* of his poetry as of his philosophizing—at every instant in which he is declaring his absorption in the divine he stands outside.

And this is what we must always keep in mind when Dante makes his ultimate claim that the poet, the vessel of inspiration, is a creator in the sense that God is. The claim must always appears absurd—even more so than it is with Longinus when he says that the sublime poet makes us think that we share the power of the gods. But it is not absurd when at the very moment he is making the claim Dante is also affirming his mere mortality. Even in saying that he is the participant in a vision he is also saying that he is apart from it and still and always in danger of abandonment—'How hard it is to tell what it was like.'[1]

---

[1] Professor Mazzeo explains Dante's view of the poet as a creator in a sympathetic way: 'Dante does not claim to create reality; he is saying rather that he can see reality, at least in part, as God sees it. The poet inspired by the Holy Spirit, the Spirit of Love and Truth, receives through the imagination truths which cannot be otherwise known or stated. Of course Dante cannot claim to see all things or to confer on any thing or *res* the status of a *signum*. He can legitimately claim, however, that, by divine inspiration, he has been able to see the God-given transcendental meanings of many of the events of his life and time. If Dante erred in claiming to use the allegory of theologians—and by all the weight of authority he did err—we are a little closer to understanding the nature of his error and why he fell into it. He erred in assuming that the allegory of theologians as understood by the doctors of the Church was a principle of construction like the allegory of poets. He did not realize that the allegory of theologians was, in the view of the interpreters of

As I see it, then, Dante's reasoning about language and poetry is as much concerned with the idea of the sublime as Longinus's, but it concludes differently because he bases his reasoning on a more definite idea of his own relationship, as an individual, to the world of divinity. His own systematizing underlies his technique, and it is therefore useful, I believe, to extend the analysis of that.

In the *Divine Comedy* no character speaks merely for himself; none has the tone or idiom of any other than Dante. Here there is not the free play of the imagination we marvel at in Shakespeare, the deliberate surrender of Euripides and Racine, the half-detachment of Dickens. It is not merely that Dante is always present in each scene, but that each character is answering questions Dante himself needs to have answered. They give the answers he must ultimately find for himself. The very vividness of Capaneus untouched by the thunderbolt, of Sordello in the midst of the gold light that lies across the grass, is the sign of the poet's own condition. In the beautiful incident of Paolo and Francesca the final pity of the story is not in their fate but in his:

> e caddi come corpo morto cade.
> > (*Inferno*, V, 142)
>
> And I fell as a dead body falls.

The point is not only that Dante fainted, but that he said he did.

Yet his characters, speaking as Dante might, still achieve their own remarkable distinctness because as individuals they are the object of the hatred of the evil in himself, hatred so complete it follows each distortion:

> La faccia sua era faccia d' uom giusto,
> tanto benigna avea di fuor la pelle,
> e d' un serpente tutto l'altro fusto.
> > (*Inferno*, XVII, 10–12)
>
> His face was the face of a just man, so mild an aspect had
> it outwardly; and the rest was all a reptile's body.

Sacred Scripture, a principle of construction only for God, not man. On the other hand, he sensed in his own vision of things a penetration, the gift of divine inspiration, which permitted him to see things and events, as God intended them to be seen, with their eternal reference and meaning' (*Structure and Thought in the Paradiso*, pp. 35–6).

They are vivid because the hatred is discriminating, and because Dante understands the evil within himself. The vividness extends to gestures, and when we see Farinata rising from his tomb, by his very silence showing his disdain of Hell, we know that Dante understands this proud contempt of Hell because he shares it. And there is the question Beatrice bitterly puts to him in Purgatory:

'Come degnasti d' accedere al monte?
non sapei tu che qui è l' uom felice?'
(*Purgatorio*, XXX, 74–5)

'How didst thou deign to draw nigh the mount?
knewest thou not that here man is happy?'

This complete fidelity in confession, this merciless attention to himself in his journey through horror and half-destroyed humanity and even in Heaven, gives us our first understanding of the man himself. Ultimately we are moved to the most noble comprehension in recognizing that this is Dante rising from a tomb, that this is also he who is defeated in a race, and that he is even like Satan, grotesquely unworthy of his role. Similarly, the sight of Matilda in the Garden of Eden is the discovery of his own capacity for delight.

What he saw in the world he saw in himself; he hated and loved as the need demanded. The reader is struck with wonder, not only at the depth of evil and the nature of its punishment, or at the splendour and tolerance of God. He is amazed at the effort of this man to judge himself.

But in all this we understand something more than self-criticism. For if Dante is in some sense Farinata, his hatred means that he is something more than the evil in Farinata. He is all that he sees, and he is something else besides; he is the judge himself. This we could not know if he did not see the others so clearly. We ourselves understand that ordinarily our own affirmations are obscure, our sincerity uncertain, and our judgments end in a blank wall. But Dante's judgments ring clear, with a clarity, I think, that comes only when a man knows his danger fully, when he accepts full responsibility for his thoughts.

Persuaded by the vividness of these scenes to recognize their validity, we are persuaded of the judgments Dante makes by recognizing ourselves in Dante, the traveller confronting himself. This goes so far, I think, that we imagine the gestures of Ciacco and Farinata to be exactly the gestures we ourselves make; in Shakespeare the gestures of Lear and Henry V are always their own, never ours. But each of these figures in the crowd of Dante's vision is also the others, and is Dante, because he knows that only in presenting the variety of Hell and Heaven will he be able to affirm himself. Given his comprehension, we are similarly committed to our own affirmations, which must for the time be Dante's, even as defined by his very gestures.

There was the danger, of course, that these galleries of souls encircling Heaven and Hell, staring at the curious visitor, the man who has imagined them out of the knowledge of his life, might yet be merely crowds of monsters we would notice and pass by. So they might be were the journey undertaken with nothing more than judgment and the idea of justice, and then we should lose something of the clarity of our perceptions and the marks of difference so finely set upon these characters. But the distinctions were preserved and the judgments vivified because there had come to this man lost in the dark wood the idea of the possibility of mercy. Each stage of the journey, each increase in the knowledge of himself, the depths of pride, the meannesses of cowardice, will make the thought, at least, his last companion.

Committed to hate evil, he retains always a kind of awe towards what is human, however wasted, an Italian rather than a Roman piety. He has no notion of disowning the friends he finds in Hell, and he promises them as if they were his kin to take back news to those who survive on earth. It is this courtesy to the damned that makes even the hatred noble. And in all that is related to Paradise he trusts his dreams, just as he trusted himself in affirming the excellence of a human being when as a child he first saw Beatrice, another child. For him, to perceive the excellence of a person was to experience love, and the years increased the depth of his loyalty. With so many causes for shame, and those constantly remembered, he never forgoes affirming the honour of that faculty which perceives excellence in another. To be permitted to know of excellence he takes to be the sign of a merciful God, the idea living in Bernard's words to the Virgin Mary:

Qui se' a noi meridiana face
  di caritate, e giuso, intra i mortali,
  se' di speranza fontana vivace.
Donna, se' tanto grande e tanto vali,
  che qual vuol grazia ed a te non ricorre,
  sua disianza vuol volar sanz' ali.
La tua benignità non pur soccorre
  a chi domanda, ma molte fiate
  liberamente al dimandar precorre.
In te misericordia, in te pietate,
  in te magnificenza, in te s' aduna
  quantunque in creatura è di bontate.
                                 (*Paradiso*, XXXIII, 10–21)

   Here art thou unto us the meridian torch of love and
there below with mortals art a living spring of hope.
   Lady, thou art so great and hast such worth, that if there
be who would have grace yet betaketh not himself to thee,
his longing seeketh to fly without wings.
   Thy kindliness not only succoureth whoso requesteth,
but doth oftentimes freely forerun request.
   In thee is tenderness, in thee is pity, in thee munificence,
in thee united whatever in created being is of excellence.

   Poetry exists in affirmation, and so does mercy, but it is not
in anyone's power to be merciful towards himself. If he is
writing religious poetry, he needs to avoid affirming his own
special worthiness or the poetry may fail to be religious. Metaphors are normally too dangerous for his purposes. When
Francis Thompson called Christ 'that great rich Vine', the
egoism of the metaphor betrayed him religiously if not poetically.
Donne, in the fourteenth of the 'Holy Sonnets', was in a sense
more successful, in identifying God as a ravisher, successful in
acknowledging his own humiliation and in showing how far that
is from humility, in acknowledging, in other words, his religious
failure. Similes are better fitted to express humility.

Lo duca mio di subito mi prese,
  come la madre ch' al romore è desta,
  e vede presso a sè le fiamme accese,
che prende il figlio e fugge e non s'arresta,
  avendo più di lui che di sè cura ...
                                 (*Inferno*, XXIII, 37–41)

My Guide suddenly took me, as a mother—that is awakened by the noise, and near her sees the kindled flames—

who takes her child and flies, caring more for him than for herself.

> Qual è colui che suo dannaggio sogna,
>   che sognando desidera sognare,
>   sì che quel ch'è, come non fosse, agogna,
> tal mi fec' io, non possendo parlare,
>   che disiava scusarmi, e scusava
>   me tuttavia, e nol mi credea fare.
>
> (Inferno, XXX, 136–41)

And as one who dreams of something hurtful to him, and dreaming wishes it were a dream, so that he longs for that which is, as if it were not:

such grew I, who, without power to speak, wished to excuse myself and all the while excused, and did not think that I was doing it.

The distance between a simile and a metaphor, as Cary Ross once described it, is as the space between two blades of grass, or between Sirius and Vega. The difference is important in understanding the conception of *The Divine Comedy* as a whole, whether it derives from an image or an idea or an encounter. The poem is not, I think, to be regarded as an allegory of a man searching for God, but, much more simply, as a construction of God's search for him. The conviction of God's existence is the truth all else refers to, and what in another philosophical construction would be an extended metaphor is here a statement of faith illustrated by a succession of similes.

Dante saw Beatrice first as a child, and then, years later, he came upon her by chance on one of the streets of Florence. He saw her seldom in life, but she came into his dreams many times and finally intervened in the Vision. In the story of the *Vita Nuova*, in all the dreams recounted there, and in *The Divine Comedy*, she appears in order to speak to him and on his behalf. It is she who seeks for him; her search has been constant and arduous:

> Quando di carne a spirto era salita,
>   e bellezza e virtù cresciuta m'era,
>   fu' io a lui men cara e men gradita;

e volse i passi suoi per via non vera,
   imagini di ben seguendo false,
   che nulla promission rendono intera.
Nè l'impetrare ispirazion mi valse,
   con le quali ed in sogno e altrimenti
   lo rivocai; sì poco a lui ne calse!
            (*Purgatorio*, XXX, 127–35)

When I was risen from flesh to spirit, and beauty and virtue were increased within me, I was less precious and less pleasing to him;
   and he did turn his steps by a way not true, pursuing false visions of good, that pay back no promise entire.
   Nor did it avail me to gain inspirations, with which in dream and otherwise, I called him back; so little recked he of them.

Her search was part of God's:

Dunque a Dio convenia con le vie sue
   riparar l' omo a sua intera vita.
            (*Paradiso*, VII, 103–4)

Wherefore needs must God with his own ways reinstate man in his unmaimed life.

There is a lithograph of Beatrice by Odilon Redon in two colours, soft yellow and pale blue, in his diffused manner. As we look at it, close or far away, the features of her face are more or less distinct, though never sharply defined. Close to, an expression becomes clear, and it is true to what we think of her. Farther away, there is merely the colour, and that seems enough. We know that none of these views is possible unless the entire painting is as it is, capable of change and yet always itself. It has the kind of constant presence Dante discovered in the original, the kind of presence we recognize in Shakerley Marmion's marvellous adaptation of Virgil:

What darkness can protect me, what disguise
Hide me from her inevitable eyes?

And in the magnificent statement of the nature of his poetry Dante acknowledged again his dependence upon some divine searching:

'I' mi son un, che quando
Amor mi spira, noto, e a quel modo
ch' e' ditta dentro vo significando.'

(*Purgatorio*, XXIV, 52-4)

The conclusion for Dante must never be—I sought for
Beatrice, or God, or mercy, and found them; but always—
through some splendid favour I became as some other. Thinking of himself, as he looked at Beatrice at the threshold of Paradise, he said:

Nel suo aspetto tal dentro mi fei,
qual si fè Glauco nel gustar de l' erba
che 'l fè consorto in mar de li altri Dei.

(*Paradiso*, I, 67-9)

Gazing on her such I became within, as was Glaucus,
tasting of the grass that made him the sea-fellow of the
other gods.

The journey of the traveller in *The Divine Comedy* is the
likeness of a journey he has in life hardly begun. When that
journey is concluded, the Dante who then joins Beatrice will
have been restored to his original self (*sua intera vita*), the self
that has hitherto been lost and confused. Dante, in this poem,
for all the inescapable personal accent, for all the emphasis
upon the search of others for him, is also saying that he does not
know himself for what he is. He sees himself in all of the damned,
and in innumerable others, they all speak in his accents, and he
holds fast to the knowledge that his only means of becoming or
restoring himself is in knowing that he is in some sense these
others. The journey is a rediscovery of the individuality that
was loved even before it existed:

Esce di mano a lui che la vagheggia
prima che sia, a guisa di fanciulla
che piangendo e ridendo pargoleggia,
l'anima semplicetta che sa nulla,
salvo che, mossa da lieto fattore,
volentier torna a ciò che la trastulla.

(*Purgatorio*, XVI, 85-90)

From his hands who fondly loves her ere she is in being,
there issues, after the fashion of a little child that sports,
now weeping, now laughing,

44

the simple, tender soul, who knoweth naught save that, sprung from a joyous maker, willingly she turneth to that which delights her.

To the reader he presents a hooded, stooped, questioning figure, more a mind than a figure, with none of the colour or brightness or darkness of a hundred others. We get hardly any picture of him except as we see him in the tortured minds of the men and women spending their punishments in eternity, or when he likens himself to some other, a child, a sea-god, a flower, or, in one of the most beautiful of all the great similes, a peasant:

> In quella parte del giovanetto anno
> che 'l sole i crin sotto l'Aquario tempra
> e già le notti al mezzo dì sen vanno,
> quando la brina in su la terra assempra
> l' imagine di sua sorella bianca,
> ma poco dura a la sua penna tempra;
> lo villanello a cui la roba manca,
> si leva, e guarda, e vede la campagna
> biancheggiar tutta, ond' ei si batte l'anca:
> ritorna in casa, e qua e là si lagna,
> come 'l tapin che non sa che si faccia;
> poi riede, e la speranza ringavagna,
> veggendo il mondo aver cangiata faccia
> in poco d' ora, e prende suo vincastro,
> e fuor le pecorelle a pascer caccia.
> Così me fece sbigottir lo mastro
> quand' io li vidi sì turbar la fronte,
> e così tosto al mal giunse lo 'impiastro;
> chè, come noi venimmo al guasto ponte,
> lo duca a me si volse con quel piglio
> dolce ch' io vidi prima a piè del monte.
>
> *(Inferno, XXIV, 1–21)*

In that part of the youthful year, when the Sun tempers his locks beneath Aquarius, and the nights already wane towards half the day,

when the hoar-frost copies his white sister's image on the ground, but short while lasts the temper of his pen,

the peasant, whose fodder fails, rises, and looks, and sees the fields all white; whereat he smites his thigh, goes back into the house, and to and fro laments like a poor wight who knows not what do do; then comes out again, and recovers hope,

observing how the world has changed its face in little time; and takes his staff, and chases forth his lambs to feed:

thus the Master made me despond, when I saw his brow so troubled; and thus quickly to the sore the plaster came.

For when we reached the shattered bridge, my Guide turned to me with that sweet aspect which I saw first at the foot of the mountain.

A similar knowledge governs his descriptions of God. It is often remarked that Dante's poetical treatment of divinity succeeds so well because of the extraordinary skill with which he uses images of light.

> Ne la profonda e chiara sussistenza
> de l'alto lume parvermi tre giri
> di tre colori e d' una contenenza;
> e l' un da l'altro come iri da iri
> parea reflesso, e 'l terzo parea foco
> che quinci e quindi igualmente si spiri.
>
> (*Paradiso*, XXXIII, 115–120)

In the profound and shining being of the deep light appeared to me three circles, of three colours and one magnitude;

one by the second as Iris by Iris seemed reflected, and the third seemed a fire breathed equally from one and from the other.

In part such images are effective because we are spared the peculiarities that usually deface an individual writer's anthropomorphism. But what is more important, I think, for the purposes of Christian religion, is that light appears to be the least corporeal of things. Difficult to think of as something concrete, it is barely adaptable for use in metaphors. I think the nature of a metaphor is in the identification of one supposed material object for another. Light cannot, I think, be used as a metaphor for God; it can only be used to describe something more like divinity than any more obviously concrete thing. Even the least corporeal of things can provide only similes of a spiritual being.

If the Christian God is not easily figured metaphorically, neither are human individuals. This is not merely because they are complex and contradictory, though such considerations are important, but primarily because their individuality is immeasurable. For any sensitive understanding, an individual conceived in character is incapable of the simplification which gives metaphors their power.

When a writer such as Dante acts upon a belief in souls he must always deal in likenesses, and not in identities of one person or thing with another. We are rather amusingly reminded of his problem when we force ourselves to remember that the persons in Hell and Purgatory are present not in body, but only as spirits. There is something incongruous, we think, in the fact that the flames are not really licking Boniface's feet as he squirms head downward in his hole. Dante means, of course, that the suffering of the soul can only be measured loosely against the suffering known to bodies. If we were to consider Hell too narrowly as a place of purely physical punishment, as we are sometimes led to do by the Doré illustrations, we should cease to take it as seriously as Dante means us to. But Dante assumes that his readers will never mistake personalities for bodies, and that they will never accept any images as the equivalents of pain or felicity. Hell and Heaven are *something* like this, he says, and he reminds us of the inexactness again and again by telling us of vision within vision, dream within dream, and by using simile after simile. His approach to the entire work, I think, in this respect, may be signified in the lines where he once speaks of himself,

> Qual è colui che somniando vede,
>   che dopo il sogno la passione impressa
>   rimane, e l' altro alla mente non riede,
> cotal son io, chè quasi tutta cessa
>   mia visione, ed ancor mi distilla
>   nel core il dolce che nacque da essa.
> (*Paradiso*, XXXIII, 58–63)

> As is he who dreaming seeth, and when the dream is gone the passion stamped remaineth, and nought else cometh to the mind again;

> even such am I; for almost wholly faileth me my vision,
> yet doth the sweetness that was born of it still drop within
> my heart.

The strength of his imagination and his feeling lead to the usual betrayal; the pictures are vivid, and we see and hear and even smell the terrible scenes as we do the very Garden of Eden. The only terms the imagination knows are concrete terms, and Dante can only present us with concrete images. The conception of the poem as a dream, a likeness, helps him not to confound his purpose, helps him in expressing the doctrine of the immeasurable vastness of the individual personality. It is immeasurable because an individual is both himself and what he sees. He is Farinata speaking as Dante and Dante speaking as Farinata. He is himself, and he is in some sense all other things.

In the thought of mercy, in thinking of himself as the object of a miraculous search, the poet undertakes to affirm the glory of whatever made him what he is. With such a purpose, poetry comes to be identified with the divine affirmation of humanity. He is endeavouring to know himself, to be true to himself: in the poem and in the philosophy he presents, it is God and Beatrice who know him and try to bring him to himself. Through his belief in them he creates himself, the grey stooped figure in its passage through dark and light; and in seeing the evil and virtue in himself he is persuaded to praise whatever made him what he was. What he is is part of what the world is, the truth of individuals, the features of a hand, the quietness of snow falling; and the life of reason in the words of the mother tongue. The world is the substance of his thought and he is part of it; the stars and land were made for him to use, to see by and to work with; and through his material and the words which mould it, the ears that hear and the eyes that see, lives the same life, from the one source. Out of that affirmation, the affirmation of love, truth speaks; and poetry comes, as an unexpected flower, *gratiosa*, out of truth.

Between the time of Longinus and Dante's century the idea of the Incarnation transformed aesthetics. The terms are often the same but the achievements are of another quality. The poetry of Dante expresses an affirmation of a different order

48

than the Platonists conceive. The man himself, and his language, are part of what he sees as well as his means of seeing. The final authority of his understanding as of his poetry is supported not only by the truth his philosophy certifies but also by the device of presenting his thought as the thought of someone he himself can stand apart from. The technique of this radical irony (integral also to the allegory) qualifies the idea Longinus had of the all-but-impersonal spectator of the mighty universe. It sacrifices something of its equanimity, but it turns what is left into something more profoundly felt, and more felt than understood.

By such a means Dante gains the intensity and conviction that are peculiar to Christian belief, a conviction one may judge to go deeper than one founded solely on the idea that it is a noble character and a noble mind that in themselves determine the character of the sublime. It is this difference, I think, that explains why the vistas are less comprehensive than those Longinus speaks of, because the focus of the Christian upon the Incarnation leads always to a concentration upon the individual and the particular, to the degree also that it exploits the idea of the terror of the individual's solitude in order to affirm the completeness of God's interest in him. That idea and that terror are equally absent from Longinus's conception of the sublime. Whether the germinal idea of the *Divine Comedy* be the idea of morning or of Paradise or of order, or still something else, he uses it not for its own interest but as the means of making the concrete and the particular vivid.

Like Longinus Dante proposes that the state of transport is a state of serenity, and in his poetry he sometimes effects this, because the pretensions of his faith are so well articulated with his understanding. And it is in the very failure of such articulation that the efforts of Michelangelo afford their astonishing contrasts. The sublime in Dante finally rests in the fulfilment of the idea of the unity of man and God, and in Michelangelo the sublime is defined as the resolution of intolerable conflicts, the contemplation of an impossible violence, and as the failure of the intellect to comprehend the idea of the Incarnation.

MICHELANGELO

IN HIS OWN TIME it was said that Michelangelo's work rivalled God's, and his force and authority are still overpowering. Sometimes he hardly seems to care about beauty, but the *terribilità*, the power and glory—this is everywhere his touch and his sign.

In what he has written he never speaks of this—what he does speak of is the work of the artist and the urgency and aspiration of love. His poems are as much a philosophy of art as they are the praise of anything, or anyone, and from them one would gather that his whole life was ridden with the torment of ambition, with the passion to achieve not merely the grandiose and monumental but the divine, as if indeed he did mean to rival God. A contemporary reported, one supposes rather faithfully, that he said substantially that: 'This sort of painting is a great undertaking', proceeded Michelangelo; 'in order to imitate to some extent the venerable image of our Lord it is not sufficient merely to be a great master in painting and very wise, but I think it is necessary for the painter to be very good in his mode of life, or even, if such were possible, a saint, so that the Holy-Spirit may inspire his intellect ... And even in the Old Testament God the Father wished that those who only had to ornament and paint the *arca foederis* should be masters not merely excellent and great, but also touched by His grace and wisdom, God saying to Moses that He would imbue them with the knowledge and intelligence of His spirit so that they might invent and do everything that He could invent and do ... Frequently images badly painted distract and cause devotion to be lost, at least in those who possess little; and, on the contrary, those that are divinely painted provoke and lead even those who are little devout and but little inclined to worship to contemplation and tears, and by their grave aspect imbue them with reverence and fear.'[1]

In the Middle Ages there was an aphorism that the inspiration of the Holy Ghost brought peace, and the Muses fury. The dove and the raven became the opposing symbols of Christian and pagan art. The Creation of Adam in the Sistine Chapel has the freshness of the Earthly Paradise and perhaps even of the first cantos of the *Paradiso* although it may not express the serenity of 'e la sua volontade è nostra pace'. But in the turmoil of the rest of the great panel there is the sublimity of passion and suffering and little enough of the peace of God. The inspiration is twofold. Now the claim of one subdues the other, and always the claim is final.

Michelangelo developed a philosophy of art that was as coherent as Dante's, and the philosophy was always part of the subject of his art. In it he sought out the authority for his ambitions, and he attempted to unite his perfect orthodoxy with the convictions of the nature of reality his Neo-Platonism certified. The *terribilità* is in part his greatness, and in part the strength of his effort to reconcile Christian and pagan truth. His poetry tells us much that helps characterize all his achievements, and it may help us determine to what degree his greatest works in their *terribilità* deserve to be thought of as sublime.

That the achievement is of the greatest order is certain. That Michelangelo's religion as well as his Neo-Platonism affects his work differently than Dante's is equally evident, as evident as the difference between his system of ideas and that of Longinus. To what degree these differences indicate a different kind of excellence is determined, I think, by the very fact that Michelangelo was inextricably committed to philosophy as such.

The Neo-Platonism of the Renaissance is generally characterized by irresponsibility, it too often accepts conclusions that are more accountable to a suffused eroticism than to reason. It begins, as all Platonism, in the most serious engagements of

---

[1] *Michelangelo Buonarroti, with translations of the Life of the Master by his Scholar, Ascanio Condivi, and Three Dialogues from the Portugese by Francisco D'Ollanda* (London, 1903), pp. 319–21 [Third Dialogue].

deductive philosophy, and it is consequently led into comprehensive and in many instances rewarding systematizing. But even at its best—in Pico and Ficino and Bruno—too often the love of truth is taken as the truth itself, and much turns out to be a mere ringing of changes on the theme of self-indulgence, an elaborate complication of egotism presented as epistemology and metaphysics.

However ridiculous and enervating at its worst, one must always take account of its value—the perfected zeal for a beautiful if not a holy life, and an enthusiasm that enthralled one noble spirit after another—Cosimo, Lorenzo, Botticelli, Michelangelo—the list never ends. And more than its influence upon lives, one must exhalt its power to determine and create styles of expression for the most ambitious artists, and to inspire particular works of superlative quality—the New Sagresty in San Lorenzo, the Primavera, the Virgin of the Rocks. What Garin says of Ficino must be said of the movement, it changed the tone of religion and morality in the sixteenth and seventeenth centuries and it renewed and redefined the sense of the beauty of the inner life.[1]

As philosophy it can be used to support religion and religiousness, and Christianity itself, but, uncontrolled, it would supplant the uniquely Christian dogmas. Sooner or later it promises immortality for certain if not all souls independently of the acts of a Creator who, incarnate as a man, offers the means of eternal felicity; and in the reverse, the distinctive exigencies of Christian dogma cannot tolerate the Platonists' arrogance: 'Notre salut n'est pas à faire, il est éternellement fait, parce qu'il fait partie de l'ordre des choses. La passion, la douleur et le péché n'ont jamais atteint que la partie inférieure de l'âme.'[2]

Michelangelo seems to have lived at the crisis of highest tension in the contrast. His work shows that from his earliest days his mind had been molded by the habits, the idiom, the tenor and limitations of the Neo-Platonic cult, and it is at the same time equally certain that from the beginning to the end of his anguish-ridden life he preserved the strictest and most passionate orthodoxy, a conservatism in faith and observance to

---

[1] Eugenio Garin, 'Ritratto di Marsilio Ficino', *Belfagor*, VI (1951), 300.
[2] Emile Bréhier, *Les Ennéades de Plotin* (Paris, 1927), IV, 215.

which the Counter-Reform presented no stress even of the slightest novelty. In drawing and in sculpture he made relatively few representations of the Crucifixion, and yet there is hardly any work of his whose subject is not intrinsically the fact and nature of it, the divine incarnated, mangled and humiliated, glorious and wasted and merciful. It is as if he thought of nothing else. The lines might have been spoken at almost every moment of his life.

> Né pinger né scolpir fie più che quieti
> l'anima, volta a quell 'amor divino
> c'aperse, a prender noi, 'n croce le braccia.

> Painting nor sculpture now can lull to rest
> My soul that turns to His great love on high
> Whose arms to clasp us on the cross were spread.[1]

The Resurrection, which he seldom represents, and, I think, never mentions in his verse, is, so to speak, in the offing. Sometimes it seems rather far distant from his immediate subject, sometimes quite close. A Neo-Platonist whose reasonings were less complicated would have had little difficulty in making it part of the background, in feeling, or in a detail of representation, and to have excluded it from the great wall paintings shows the extent of the preoccupation with the idea of the Crucifixion, the Sacrifice. But this is Michelangelo's form, as a Neo-Platonist and as a Christian—he will represent life up to the point of death, and death, and not the moment after: the conflict, the suffering, the sacrifice, all those images of the using up and devouring of life which he presents so fully, and egotistically, and beyond that the most he will do is to affirm, often in verse, and often in the Pietàs, the need of the Resurrected God and his faith in Him, but not the fact in itself. Even the

---

[1] Michelangiolo Buonarroti, *Rime*, ed. E. N. Girardi (Bari, 1960), no. 285. The translation is by J. A. Symonds, *The Sonnets of Michael Angelo Buonarroti* (London, 1926), no. LXV. Although Symonds's translations are based on the Guasti text of 1863, I have used them wherever there are no differences in the Girardi text that would require significantly different interpretations. When there are such differences, and they are infrequent, I supply other translations.

Michelangelo's poems are often so difficult to understand that one can hardly expect any translation to answer all the questions the text presents. Symonds's poems should perhaps be thought of as readings rather than translations, and as such they continue to command respect.

Rondanini Pietà shows no abrogation of the faith though it seems to confront a life as horrible as Belsen—

> Già fur gli occhi nostri interi
> con la luce in ogni speco;
> or son voti, orrendi e neri ...
>
> (21)

Once our eyes were full of light throughout the pupil; now they are empty, hideous and black—this is what time has done.

And wonderfully enough, in him it is also the faith of the Neo-Platonist—the faith of the pagan helps the Christian consolidate his strength.

A man who had seen Michelangelo working said that 'He went at the marble with such an impetus and fury as to make me believe that the entire work was going to pieces. With a single stroke he would split off morsels of three or four inches in thickness.'[1] Cellini's comment was that 'he was often seized by many awesome furies that came over him as he worked',[2] and one would judge this to be his temperament in everything he did. And in the poems one judges that the character of his love was much as the character of his approach to stone and paint and verse.

He himself speaks of the relationship between an artist and his material in terms that are parallel to those that describe the way of love:

> Se ben concetto ha la divina parte
> il volto e gli atti d'alcun, po' di quello
> doppio valor con breve e vil modello
> dà vita a' sassi, e non è forza d'arte.

---

[1] Blaise De Vigenère, *Les Images ou tableaux de la plate Peinture* (Paris, 1614), p. 885. I owe this reference and the translation to R. J. Clements, 'Michelangelo on Effort and Rapidity in Art', *Journal of the Warburg and Courtauld Institutes*, XVII (1954), 304.

[2] *Due Trattati* (Milan, 1811), p. 213. This may be judged to be a matter of temperament, without particular significance, or it may be taken as evidence of inspiration and possession, as I suppose Lomazzo would have it: 'E fra gl' altri giudico che 'l pittore non dia mai di piglio al penello se non quando sente eccitarsi da vn natural furore, il qual non è dubio che cosi corre ne' pittori come ne' poeti, ne si astringa mai à farlo à commandamento altrui, per che non è possibile che possa farsi alcun' opera lodeuole à dispetto delle muse, le quali troppo si sdegnano di essere mandate à vettura' (*Trattato dell' Arte della Pittura, Scoltura, et Architettura* [Milan, 1585], p. 484).

Né altrimenti in più rustiche carte,
anz'una pronta man prenda 'l pennello,
fra ' dotti ingegni il più accorto e bello
pruova e rivede, e suo storie comparte.

   Simil di me model di poca istima
mie parto fu, per cosa alta e prefetta
da voi rinascer po', donna alta e degna.

   Se 'l poco accresce, e 'l mie superchio lima
vostra mercé, qual penitenzia aspetta
mie fiero ardor, se mi gastiga e 'nsegna?

(236)

When that which is divine in us doth try
   To shape a face, both brain and hand unite
   To give, from a mere model frail and slight,
   Life to the stone by Art's free energy.
Thus too before the painter dares to ply
   Paint-brush or canvas, he is sent to write
   Sketches on scraps of paper, and invite
   Wise minds to judge his figured history.
So, born a model rude and mean to be
   Of my poor self, I gain a nobler birth,
   Lady, from you, you fountain of all worth!
Each overplus and each deficiency
   You will make good. What penance then is due
   For my fierce heat, chastened and taught by you?
(Symonds, XIV—*second reading*)

Such working of art and love, if not described as fury or the onset of demons, is nevertheless compared to the consuming of fire, at once a devouring and a purification:

Sol pur col foco il fabbro il ferro stende
al concetto suo caro e bel lavoro,
né senza foco alcuno artista l'oro
al sommo grado suo raffina e rende;

   né l'unica fenice sé riprende
se non prim'arsa; ond'io, s'ardendo moro,
spero più chiar resurger tra coloro
che morte accresce e 'l tempo non offende.

   Del foco, di ch'i' parlo, ho gran ventura
c'ancor per rinnovarmi abbi in me loco,
sendo già quasi nel numer de' morti.

55

O ver, s'al cielo ascende per natura,
al suo elemento, e ch'io converso in foco
sie, come fie che seco non mi porti?

(62)

It is with fire that blacksmiths iron subdue
      (*translating a different first line*)
  Unto fair form, the image of their thought:
Nor without fire hath any artist wrought
  Gold to its utmost purity of hue.
Nay, nor the unmatched phœnix lives anew,
  Unless she burn: if then I am distraught
  By fire, I may to better life be brought
  Like those whom death restores nor years undo.
The fire whereof I speak, is my great cheer;
  Such power it hath to renovate and raise
  Me who was almost numbered with the dead;
And since by nature fire doth find its sphere
  Soaring aloft, and I am all ablaze,
  Heavenward with it my flight must needs be sped.

(LIX)

As any Neo-Platonist, and any Christian, he wants to assert the primacy of love, in God, in God the Creator, in the Created, and he has the need to assert of his own work that it shares in and derives from divinity. His thought will take many directions in supporting the analogy, and at times he will explore ideas that do more to confuse than certify it, but the intensity of his love, for the meaning of his art as for those he loves, the wholeness of the dedication, the concentration of his egotism, all require the reasoning that will justify the wholeness of the effort and the sacrifice of life to its effects. The affirmations that follow his commitment are almost obsessional. The act of loving, in every sphere, becomes an act either of engendering or conceiving, the life of the artist is a life of gestation. In love as in art, the lover loses himself in what he loves or makes; his gestation, his creation, is a dying to himself and a rebirth in another, a newly created and immortal life—in the Platonic way:

model di poca istima
mie parto fu, per cosa alta e prefetta
da voi rinascer po', donna alta e degna.

(236)

born of a model of little worth, I am reborn through you,
O noble and virtuous Lady, through so lofty and perfect
a thing.

Nevertheless, it is the purpose and the intention that he
tries never to forget, however much the idea of travail absorbs
him—all is hopefully for the sake of a new creation.

Longinus's idea that the poet and his readers, in a state of
elevation, suppose for a while they are taking part in the
creating processes of Nature itself seems more a figure of speech
than a belief when one confronts it with Michelangelo's argument to demonstrate that the process of engendering in nature
is also the process of the imagination itself in bringing its works
into being.

In one of his greatest poems Michelangelo says that the
labour of a lifetime finally resulted in an achievement that was
true to his intention. And he says that what was such long
travail with him was the same as the process with Nature herself who, after so many ages, fashioned 'you'. 'And as I look on
your face', he said (I am paraphrasing), 'I do not know whether
to be sad or joyful, seeing that it is at the end of my life that
this perfection is attained—whether to be sad or joyful because
this is the end; or whether to be sad at the sight of such perfection; or to be filled with joy at it.'

> Negli anni molti e nelle molte pruove,
> cercando, il saggio al buon concetto arriva
> d'un'immagine viva,
> vicino a morte, in pietra alpestra e dura;
> c'all'alte cose nuove
> tardi si viene, e poco poi si dura.
> Similmente natura,
> di tempo in tempo, d'uno in altro volto,
> s'al sommo, errando, di bellezza è giunta
> nel tuo divino, è vecchia, e de' perire:
> onde la tema, molto
> con la beltà congiunta,
> di stranio cibo pasce il gran desire;
> né so pensar né dire
> qual nuoca o giovi più, visto 'l tuo 'spetto,
> o 'l fin dell'universo o 'l gran diletto.

(241)

After searching many years and after many trials, only when he is near death is the artist on the point of giving life, through rough, hard stone, to the lofty idea that is in his mind; for he comes late to new and lofty ideas and when but little of life remains to him. So nature, too, in its wanderings through time, passing from one countenance to another, comes finally to the making of thy face, the very perfection of beauty, but by then nature, too, is old and ready to die.

This is why the fear of death, so closely bound to beauty, feeds my great yearning with strange food, and, watching you, I neither know how to think or to say what gives me the greatest pleasure—the feeling of the approaching end of the world, or my great delight in the sight of you.

The artist who has arrived at the conception of a living image communicates its very life to the stone he is working with, just as Nature in her creation gives life to her children.

What is at issue is what Vasari speaks of in praising Donatello: 'For the Guild of Armourers, Donatello executed a most animated figure of St George, in his armour. The brightness of youthful beauty, generosity, and bravery shine forth in his face; his attitude gives evidence of a proud and terrible impetuosity; the character of the saint is indeed expressed most wonderfully, and life seems to move within that stone.'[1]

No more than Donatello did Michelangelo suppose his work would cause the life within the stone to move. I do not even suppose that his speculation would lead him as far as Henri Focillon goes: 'Life is form, and form is the modality of life. The relationships that bind forms together in nature cannot be pure chance, and what we call "natural life" is in effect a relationship between forms, so inexorable that without it this natural life could not exist. So it is with art as well. The formal relationships within a work of art and among different works of art constitute an order for, and a metaphor of, the entire universe ... It is my conviction that [plastic] forms constitute an order of existence, and that this order has the motion and breath of life.'[2]

[1] *Lives of Seventy of the Most Eminent Painters*, translated by E. H. and E. W. Blashfield and A. A. Hopkins (New York, 1896), I, 313.
[2] *The Life of Forms in Art*, translated by C. B. Hogan and George Kubler (New Haven, 1942), pp. 2 and 6.

It would seem that a tradition that comes from Plotinus and Augustine would offer the strongest support to Michelangelo's aspiration. According to Plotinus the life of a living organism issues from its illumination by the soul (I. 1. 10), and the life of all animals from an illumination of the universal soul (I. 1. 11). Since the most perfect life of the soul is the act of intelligence (I. 1. 13), it has the power as such of informing things with the life it itself possesses, so moving and shaping them that it gives them form. The life in a work of art acts just as does the life in a living body: the life of the body is the life of a dancer, and its motions are an image of the life that has brought him into being (III. 2. 16). These two ideas—that of the light of the intelligence, and that of a work of art as an image of life itself— would confirm Michelangelo's assertions that he is indeed conferring life upon what he works with—they would confirm, although I do not think it can be claimed that they justify the assertion.

Augustine is somewhat more specific in his remarks on the creativity of the artist although the essential idea is the same. He speaks of rhythm as the element that finally determines the presence of life in art as in living things. A statue, he says, does not possess all the harmony and rhythm (*numerositas*) possessed by a human body, but that which it does possess it derives from the wisdom of the artist, which in turn derives from his creator. How one is to take the phrase '*all* the rhythm and harmony' I do not know, but his way of saying this may also be thought to support Michelangelo, maintaining merely a difference of degree in the creations of Nature and of art.[1]

Michelangelo says that the sculptor gives life to stone. The process itself he likens to gestation although he may have been thinking in terms better characterized as metempsychosis. He is careful to make it clear that this is what he regards as a process that is always taking place in nature. The love that has urged the artist towards his work is part of the great dynamism of the universe, conceiving and creating into eternity. The creation of the artist is indeed a continuation of the creation of God—the impulse is the same, the informing purpose is the same.

[1] *De Diversis Quaestionibus LXXXIII*, LXXVIII (*Patrologia Latina*, XL, 89–90). Comparable reasoning by Plotinus (I. 6. 2; v. 8. 1; V. 9. 3) is examined by Karel Svoboda, *L'Esthétique de Saint Augustin et ses Sources* (Brno, 1933), p. 115.

And still the essential difficulty remains. Perhaps it is Bruno who has the only solution for the Neo-Platonists—a work of art is indeed a work such as God's, but with this difference: 'as soon as it is finished it is abandoned by its author, who no longer lives in it. The work of nature, on the contrary, being the product of the universal intellect which is here designated by the compelling term "internal artist" (*da noi si chiama artefice interno*), never becomes detached from the creative principle always present in it and in each of its parts and which gives it life.'[1]

In the midst of difficulties of so confounding a kind, a natural conclusion—if not a solution—will be that the creations of an artist are ideal and abstract rather than concrete or organic. His moulding of materials will be not for the sake of the material or of life but for the ideal, a creation of the mind sharing the reality of the mental life in some fusion of abstraction and beauty and generality, this at least to be certified as genuinely the individual's creation:

> Amore è un concetto di bellezza
> immaginata o vista dentro al core,
> amica di virtute e gentilezza.

(38)

Love is an idea of beauty, imagined or seen within the heart, the friend of virtue and nobleness.

Just as the figures of the New Sagresty and the Slaves and almost all the others are one might say the portraits of transcendentals, it is the ideal or its discovery that is the creative action of the mind, and the artist, as the lover, is engaged in the love of the ideal, not of what one might try to think of as simply corporeal or living or powerful, but what in some ideal way has as fixed and defined a form and existence as the object that portrays it.

But here, too, the claim for a power like God's is elusive— it is the general, the ideal, that has come to life, what by definition is every rational creature's, not strictly an individual creation at all—what is individual is the stone itself as it is

---

[1] From a paraphrase by Paul-Henri Michel of Bruno's *De la causa, principio et uno* in 'Renaissance Cosmologies', *Diogenes*, no. 18 (Summer, 1957), p. 99.

shaped, or the words, or the image of the beloved in the lover's mind.[1]

And yet, the artist has some right to the claim of generation— no one else will ever create or manifest the ideal he has brought to light. It is in short the thing *seen*, the representation of the image within his mind, that is his peculiar production—not the *concetto*, but the *imagine*. The *concetto*—exactly as in Longinus —has laid hold upon him and through the power of its enthrallment creates an image, an image deriving from itself:

> Non ha l'ottimo artista alcun concetto
> c'un marmo solo in sé non circonscriva
> col suo superchio, e solo a quello arriva
> la man che ubbidisce all'intelletto.
>
> (151)

> The best of artists hath no thought to show
>   Which the rough stone in its superfluous shell
>   Doth not include: to break the marble spell
> Is all the hand that serves the brain can do.
>   (XV)

One may see the parallel and contrast with Longinus at every step of the argument. A single force moves through all things—this is in both of them—but Longinus says that men, elevated by the power of poetry and thought, become spectators of the mighty whole, and are ecstatic, whereas Michelangelo says their fulfilment is in participating, through the imagination and with tools, in the continuing creations of Nature, in the processes of bringing to birth, of being born, and of dying.

The idea of the artist as creator, by the terms of the Neo-Platonic paradox, is also the idea that creation is merely the discovery of the self. The love of God is identical with the love of self, and the process of creating, as of loving, is the same as the act of knowing. The fact that this is paradox absorbs Michelangelo quite as much as the doctrine it embodies.

[1] Here, I think, one should observe that the Neo-Platonist philosophers made an effort to claim that the idea of a particular thing in the mind—a table, for example —was not a specific picture of a table, but something generic. Ficino, for example, in commenting on Plotinus, goes out of his way to make the point (*Opera* [1576], p. 1644).

Michelangelo so strongly felt the attraction of the beautiful that his mind and all his being seemed to move immediately to possess it. 'It was not only the beauty of human beings that he loved, he loved every beautiful thing, "con maraviglioso affetto".'¹ And in what are reported to us as his own words:

Whenever I see someone who possesses virtue, who displays an agile mind, who knows how to do or say something better than others, I am forced to fall in love with him.²

As always with Michelangelo, philosophy could be used to support the authority of love, for it could be shown to lead to the love of God and to the love of God within the self. Arrogating to itself the quality of divinity, it would turn even defeat into victory. And religion also was brought to its support. There is an interesting letter which a certain Frate Lorenzo delle Colombe wrote to Michelangelo in 1516 in words that might have been the artist's own:

Thou knowest that neither time nor place can put an end to love, least of all God's love; and more, too, love transforms one into the other, the lover into what he loves, and makes a mutual interpenetration of souls. And therefore, from the love I bear thee, being within thee, I penetrate thy inmost parts and I understand what thou art thinking and saying and writing ... Let us love each other then, in the Lord, as we have done heretofore, and we shall know and understand all things, and truth itself, and we shall see it face to face, if we live well and as Christians. Meanwhile, prepare to sculpture within thy soul, with the hammer of good and virtuous works, the imprint of Christ who was crucified for us, all which should be done in faith and through faith inspired by holy charity ...³

This is indeed the old Platonic and Petrarchan doctrine in Christian terms, 'l'amante ne l'amato si transforme',⁴ the

¹ Ascanio Condivi, *Vita di Michelangiolo* (Florence, 1944), p. 97.

² *Dialogi di Donato Giannotti, De' Giorni che Dante Consumò nel cercare l'Inferno e 'l Purgatorio*, ed. D. Redig de Campos (Florence, 1939), p. 68.

Adrian Stokes has analysed this trait in Freudian terms, and he relates it to another, Michelangelo's desire to lead a hermit's existence. He makes the point that Michelangelo needed to resist this continuous impulsion to sympathize with things outside himself if he was to maintain the privacy he needed for the cultivation of his inner life (*Michelangelo*, [London, 1955], pp. 128–9).

³ Translated from the transcription of Charles De Tolnay, *The Youth of Michelangelo* (Princeton, 1947), p. 252.

⁴ *Trionfo d'Amore*, l. 162 (*Rime*, ed. Chiorboli, p. 318). Ficino uses the same words, 'amor amantem transferens in amatum' (*Argumentum in Sextam Epistolam* [*Opera*, p. 1534]).

lover is transformed into the loved one. The idea is in the *Phaedrus*, and wherever there is the doctrine that where your heart is, there will your treasure be;[1] it is in the Aristotelian psychology Dante uses at almost every point where the sinner or the virtuous soul becomes transformed into the likeness of his adulation. But there is a particular bent to the idea in Michelangelo that is specially Petrarchan as well as religious, the changing of the lover into the very person of the beloved—'l 'immedisimarsi dell'amante nella persona amata'.[2]

F. M. Bongianni does better than the Freudians, I think, in referring this matter of the identification with the beloved to Michelangelo's religion. He remarks, for example, that Michelangelo's love for Tommaso de' Cavalieri and Vittoria Colonna is for him a means of rediscovering the destiny of his own soul, even though, paradoxically, he speaks of it as a loss of his own identity in theirs.

[1] Plotinus's expression of the idea puts it at the centre of his philosophy: ' ... in contemplative vision, especially when it is vivid, we are not at the time aware of our own personality; we are in possession of ourselves, but the activity is towards the object of vision with which the thinker becomes identified; he has made himself over as matter to be shaped; he takes ideal form under the action of the vision while remaining, potentially, himself. This means that he is actively himself when he has intellection of nothing' (*Enneads*, IV. 4.2—MacKenna's translation).

Ficino is entirely in harmony with Plotinus when he develops the idea to this point: you become what you love because, ultimately, the divine makes you into its own likeness (*Theologiæ Platonicæ*, XII, i [*Opera*, p. 265]). For him this idea finally becomes explicitly mystical and Christian: 'The inner man is daily renewed, and the invisible and the eternal are revealed to us—as we look upon the glory of God we see His face, and we ourselves are transformed into His likeness, splendour by splendour' (XIV, ii [*Opera*, p. 309]).

Leonardo was similarly involved with certain phases of this doctrine, as Giuseppina Fumagalli has explained in her *Eros di Leonardo* (Milan, 1952), pp. 209–25.

[2] G. G. Ferrero, *Il Petrarchismo del Bembo e le Rime di Michelangelo* (Turin, 1935), p. 69.

The way Annibale Romei puts it, speaking of the identification as something accomplished 'spiritalmente', points up the violence with which Michelangelo pursues what in another might be spoken of as simply metaphor, but what must in his thought be regarded as the very issue of the Neo-Platonic philosophy: 'Each time our soul imagines something it takes on its likeness, and in a spiritual sense it becomes the thing it has imagined. And what is true of the senses is also true of the intellect, for feeling and understanding are alike in all respects. When the intellect understands something and contemplates what it understands, it becomes that very thing. Truly they are blessed who apply the lovely gift of the mind to the contemplation of what is lofty and divine because in that itself they attain divinity' (*Discorsi* [Pavia, 1591], p. 82 [*Giornata Seconda: Dell' Amore Humano*]).

D'altrui pietoso e sol di sé spietato
nasce un vil bruto, che con pena e doglia
l'altrui man veste e la suo scorza spoglia
e sol per morte si può dir ben nato.

Così volesse al mie signor mie fato
vestir suo viva di mie morta spoglia,
che, come serpe al sasso si discoglia,
pur per morte potria cangiar mie stato.

O fussi sol la mie l'irsuta pelle
che, del suo pel contesta, fa tal gonna
che con ventura stringe sì bel seno,

ch'i' l'are' pure il giorno; o le pianelle
che fanno a quel di lor basa e colonna,
ch'i' pur ne porterei duo nevi almeno.

(94)

Kind to the world, but to itself unkind,
   A worm is born, that dying noiselessly
   Despoils itself to clothe fair limbs, and be
   In its true worth by death alone divined.
Oh, would that I might die, for her to find
   Raiment in my outworn mortality!
   That, changing like the snake, I might be free
   To cast the slough wherein I dwell confined!
Nay, were it mine, that shaggy fleece that stays,
   Woven and wrought into a vestment fair,
   Around her beauteous bosom in such bliss!
All through the days she'd clasp me! Would I were
   The shoes that bear her burden! When the ways
   Were wet with rain, her feet I then should kiss!

(XXI)

Michelangelo speaks of a worm becoming a butterfly and of a serpent's changing its skin as a preparation for the expression of his desire that his own skin should become the skin of his beloved. This is more than the Petrarchan metaphor, for it also signifies salvation: ' ... renewed through the experience of another's individuality, and all the while still most intimately conscious of his own being, the poet believes that the labour of his love promises to achieve that satisfaction, and indeed that masterpiece, that he despairs of in his present life and by the very fact of his individuality ... We do not achieve our work as mere individuals engaged in serving our ordinary interests, but through serving the Good that joins us to itself.'[1] Bongianni means to say that we are to think of all such ideas of meta-morphosis as conversion.

What gives all this such extraordinary intensity is the actuality of the process as Michelangelo conceives it, the transforma-tion of the body as well as of the soul. There is in the very idea an urgency that distinguishes Michelangelo's thought from all gentlemanly Neo-Platonizing, and even from the most responsible Platonists. It may be true, as Garin says, that Ficino's Platonism is an elaborate answer to a despair he cannot endure, and that for him therefore beauty is also a means of conversion, a conversion of the soul to divine existence.[2] But the despair that is part and parcel of Michelangelo's faith I think is more appropriately to be compared with Pascal's than Ficino's. In at once seeking and fleeing solitude he seeks and flees annihi-lation as well as God. As Bongianni says, he thinks of his life as part of the history of humanity, always awaiting the Apocalypse that will never come because it is outside history.[3] The Apoca-lypse and the Resurrection.

But the poems do not always express the violence and des-peration of the desire, sometimes there is something much more like peace, as if there were at least a sight of fulfilment. So it is, I think, in the beautiful and moving sonnet in which the poet imagines he succeeds in seeing with the beloved's eyes:

> Veggio co' be' vostr'occhi un dolce lume
> che co' mie ciechi già veder non posso;
> porto co' vostri piedi un pondo addosso,
> che de' mie zoppi non è già costume.
>
> Volo con le vostr'ale senza piume;
> col vostro ingegno al ciel sempre son mosso;
> dal vostro arbitrio son pallido e rosso,
> freddo al sol, caldo alle più fredde brume.
>
> Nel voler vostro è sol la voglia mia,
> i miei pensier nel vostro cor si fanno,
> nel vostro fiato son le mie parole.
>
> Come luna da sé sol par ch'io sia,
> ché gli occhi nostri in ciel veder non sanno
> se non quel tanto che n'accende il sole.　(89)

[1] 'Sul travaglio religioso di Michelangelo', *Rivista di Sintesi Letteraria*, II (1935), 284.
[2] *L'Umanesimo Italiano* (Bari, 1952), p. 129.
[3] 'Sul travaglio religioso di Michelangelo', p. 274.

With your fair eyes a charming light I see,
    For which my own blind eyes would peer in vain;
    Stayed by your feet the burden I sustain
    Which my lame feet find all too strong for me;
Wingless upon your pinions forth I fly;
    Heavenward your spirit stirreth me to strain;
    E'en as you will I blush and blanch again,
    Freeze in the sun, burn 'neath a frosty sky.
Your will includes and is the lord of mine;
    Life to my thoughts within your heart is given;
    My words begin to breathe upon your breath:
Like to the moon am I, that cannot shine
    Alone; for lo! our eyes see nought in heaven
    Save what the living sun illumineth.

                            (XXX)[1]

The idea of becoming what one loves, of reaching forth to take on another's identity, is a significant paradox for the Neo-Platonists, committed as they also are to the cultivation of the inner self, to finding God and truth within themselves, and in their very psychology of the imagination committed to adoring the image that is within them:

> Amore è un concetto di bellezza
> immaginata o vista dentro al core,
> amica di virtute e gentilezza.

                                 (38)

Love is an idea of beauty, imagined or seen within the heart, friend to virtue and nobility.

Looking into the eyes of the beloved, Michelangelo said he found perfect peace, 'intera pace'; and in the same breath, that he felt love in the very likeness of his own soul, deep within and all holy

> dentro, ov'ogni mal dispiace,
> chi d'amor l'alma a sé simil m'assale.

                                 (105)

Within, where every impure thought displeases, I beheld Him who clothes my soul with the love that makes it like unto Him.

---

[1] The idea of seeing with another's eyes is part of the idea in Ficino that in loving God one comes to see with His eyes. *Theologiæ Platonicæ*, XII, i (*Opera*, p. 267); *Epistolae, Liber* IIII (*Opera*, p. 772).

The conceit and the paradox are meant to be a solution to explain how it is one may love another than oneself.[1]

And there were, one supposes, rare instants where the peace, the attainment of what he strove for so furiously, came beneficently, seeking him out, and leaving him with the conviction that he had come to rest in truth itself.

In a certain fragment Michelangelo wrote of his original sight of absolute beauty, speaking of it as something the soul received through the eyes. (He may be saying that this beauty first appeared to him as he looked at his beloved, but this is not the necessary condition of the statement.) The power of the beauty was such that the image of it that was formed in his mind grew to such brightness it quite overpowered the soul.

The next thought of the fragment prepares for a conclusion that we cannot now certainly anticipate: the god of love saw his amazement and smiled; and then the god returned (I suppose, from occasioning this event) to the side of the lover, meaning to see to it that the lover should not undo what had been effected.

The complexity of possibilities is now such that one hardly knows who is on whose side—the lover's, love, beauty, the soul, but there seems to be an implication that the soul in partnership with love possesses an excellence that cannot tolerate ravishment even by absolute beauty:

> Mentre c'alla beltà ch'i' vidi in prima
> appresso l'alma, che per gli occhi vede,
> l'immagin dentro cresce, e quella cede
> quasi vilmente e senza alcuna stima.
>   Amor, c'adopra ogni suo ingegno e lima,
> perch'io non tronchi 'l fil ritorna e riede.

(44)

[1] Leonardo explains the doctrine step by step: 'The lover is drawn by the thing loved, as the sense is by that which it perceives, and it unites with it and they become one and the same thing. The work is the first thing born of the union; if the thing that is loved be base, the lover becomes base. When the thing taken into union is in harmony with that which receives it, there follow rejoicing and pleasure and satisfaction. When the lover is united to that which is loved it finds rests there; when the burden is laid down there it finds rest. The thing is known with our intellect' (translated by Edward MacCurdy, *The Notebooks of Leonardo da Vinci* [New York, 1955], pp. 66–7. The passage is from the *Codice Trivulziano*, and is transcribed by Giuseppina Fumagalli, *Leonardo Omo Sanza Lettere*, (Florence, 1952), p. 349.

In saying that the image can grow until it takes possession of all one's being, the poet seems to be rejecting the authority of the imagination, and to insist upon the nobility of other phases of his life, perhaps in particular, the necessary relation of the soul to truth and goodness, and thus is insisting on the authority of reason and virtue. The final emphasis is on the marriage of the mind with truth.[1]

The idea of the artist as creator naturally leads to the consideration of the distinctions that are to be made between what goes on within the mind and what goes on outside. In one aspect Michelangelo approaches the problem whenever he opposes *concetto* and *imagine* on the one side—the glorious or, as the case may be, blinding ideal itself—and on the other, that which has a concrete and living existence in the mind of the beholder of the ideal, its image.

He uses the same word for the image within his mind and the representations of his painting and sculpture, and it does not seem that he considers there to be a radical difference in the nature of the two kinds of image. He is as much absorbed in the mystery of his imagination as in that of art, although the latter as a subject for meditation often leads him into more elaborate analysis. The analogy of the artist with the creating God in particular brings out his fullest and clearest statements as he tries to show the likeness of the creation that takes place in the mind with that outside it. Michelangelo is consistent in maintaining that the key factor is the operation of divine power, and he will even speak of it as 'grace', in painting and in sculpture as well as in the forming of the image in the mind:

[1] The idea of an image possessing the power to fascinate and drive from the mind all else provides the beginning of another sonnet:

> Non posso altra figura immaginarmi
> o di nud' ombra o di terrestre spoglia,
> col più alto pensier, tal che mie voglia
> contra la tuo beltà di quella s'armi.
>
> (82)

> I cannot by the utmost flight of thought
>   Conceive another form of air or clay,
>   Wherewith against thy beauty to array
>   My wounded heart in armour fancy-wrought.
>
> (XXVII)

Se 'l mie rozzo martello i duri sassi
forma d'uman aspetto or questo or quello,
dal ministro che 'l guida, iscorge e tiello,
prendendo il moto, va con gli altrui passi.
   Ma quel divin che in cielo alberga e stassi,
altri, e sé più, col propio andar fa bello;
e se nessun martel senza martello
si può far, da quel vivo ogni altro fassi.

(46)

When my rude hammer to the stubborn stone
   Gives human shape, now that, now this, at will,
   Following his hand who wields and guides it still,
   It moves upon another's feet alone:
But that which dwells in heaven, the world doth fill
   With beauty by pure motions of its own;
   And since tools fashion tools which else were none,
   Its life makes all that lives with living skill.

(LXI)

The power of the artist at another place is spoken of as
deriving from the artist's contemplation of heavenly beauty, a
power which is itself inadequate without grace:

Per fido esemplo alla mia vocazione
nel parto mi fu data la bellezza,
che d'ambo l'arti m'è lucerna e specchio.
S'altro si pensa, è falsa opinione.
Questo sol l'occhio porta a quella altezza
c'a pingere e scolpir qui m'apparecchio.
   S'e' giudizi temerari e sciocchi
al senso tiran la beltà, che muove
e porta al cielo ogni intelletto sano,
dal mortale al divin non vanno gli occhi
infermi, e fermi sempre pur là d'ove
ascender senza grazia è pensier vano.

(164)

The beauty that gives me light and is the model of both
the arts I practise was given me at birth as the faithful
guide for my vocation. If anyone thinks otherwise of my
work he is wrong, for it is beauty alone that can raise the
sight to those lofty conceptions that I labour to paint and
carve. If bold, foolish men think that beauty, which moves
every sane intellect and transports it to heaven itself, is
born of the senses, let them know that our weak vision

cannot of itself ascend from the mortal to the divine, but remains always below. For it is vain to think that it can be raised without the help of grace.

Michelangelo is here saying that beauty exists in potentiality in the inmost spirit and after that in the actualization of the artist's work—beauty which comes to be part of the soul, is made concrete there, as an image, and later it is embodied in things that can be seen and touched and heard.[1] And all this, depending upon the mind's being carried up to heaven, would come about, and no fulfilment of the desire to create would be granted—indeed the thought itself would be vain—if it were not that grace permitted the ascent.

He might have left it at this, using the idea of grace as a mere metaphor for light, or taking up with any of the other devices of the Neo-Platonists that ascribe divinity to the processes of the mind. But in the very sonnet in which he speaks of his mallet as being guided by a divine hand, he presents a Christian idea that goes beyond anything a Platonic theory would assert, where he declares that an angel, and no mere spirit, but the angelic being of a once mortal person, Vittoria Colonna, is the instrument of God's use of him. In almost anyone else one would speak of this as preciosity, but here the very particularity of the Christian idea relates the idea of creation by an artist to the most mysterious phase of all in the theory of creation, the creating of the individual and the concrete.

> E perché 'l colpo è di valor più pieno
> quant'alza più se stesso alla fucina,
> sopra 'l mie questo al ciel n'è gito a volo.
>   Onde a me non finito verrà meno,
> s'or non gli dà la fabbrica divina
> aiuto a farlo, c'al mondo era solo.   (46)

> Now, for that every stroke excels the more
>   The higher at the forge it doth ascend,
>   Her soul that fashioned mine hath sought the skies:
> Wherefore unfinished I must meet my end,
>   If God, the great artificer, denies
>   That aid which was unique on earth before.
>   (LXI)

[1] One may here compare Ficino's commentary on the *Philebus*: 'nothing bears fruition in the outer world unless it has first given birth within' (*Opera*, p. 1226).

The claim to create as God does, giving life, and even fashioning individuals, is one thing if it is thought to be within the comprehension and justification of philosophy, but it is quite another when it includes the claim of being able to create what is corporal and unique. It is the particular work of art, at the particular time of its creation, that is taken as the demonstration of the justice of the analogy with God, but the claim falters badly when the artist claims that the material of his work—the stone, words, colour—are also his creation. And yet there is no part of the aspiration Michelangelo clings to more tenaciously.

He was supported in this, of course, by his temperament. It was well remarked that 'his whole soul drew whatever was bodily and corporal to it as to its own'.[1] One might well believe that it is this disposition that caused him to put aside the reasoning of Ficino and Diacceto, his own teacher, whereby one conceived of love as a series of steps leading to the ultimate absorption: 'for this he substituted the idea of the closest relationship between lover and loved one, a relationship so close it would itself be conceived of as the hammer that gave new form to the substance, otherwise inert, of the lover'.[2] This would be part and parcel of his famous *senso delle cose* which as much as anything accounts for the peculiar characteristics of his language. And it is this trait that has been said to explain how he can substitute the figure of the angel, who was Vittoria Colonna, for the Platonic schematization. He went contrary to the dominant expression of the problem in Neo-Platonism by this very concreteness, not forgetting or suppressing in the process of abstraction the reality of the individual, whose peculiar function it could be, in being loved, to transform the lover.[3] And it is this trait, signally defined in the sonnet 'se 'l mie rozzo martello' (46), that helps provide the interpretation for his most famous and possibly most profound statement on the nature of artistic and divine creation.

> Non ha l'ottimo artista alcun concetto
> c'un marmo solo in sé non circonscriva
> col suo superchio, e solo a quello arriva
> al man che ubbidisce all'intelletto.

[1] Arturo Farinelli, *Michelangelo e Dante* (Turin, 1918), p. 28.
[2] Luigi Baldacci, 'Lineamenti della Poesia di Michelangelo', *Paragone*, no. 72 (December, 1955), p. 36.
[3] Ibid., p. 36.

Il mal ch'io fuggo, e 'l ben ch'io mi prometto,
in te, donna leggiadra, altera e diva,
tal si nasconde; e perch'io più non viva,
contraria ho l'arte al disïato effetto.
    Amor dunque non ha, né tua beltate
o durezza o fortuna o gran disdegno
del mio mal colpa, o mio destino o sorte;
    se dentro del tuo cor morte e pietate
porti in un tempo, e che 'l mio basso ingegno
non sappia, ardendo, trarne altro che morte.

(151)

The best of artists hath no thought to show
    Which the rough stone in its superfluous shell
    Doth not include: to break the marble spell
    Is all the hand that serves the brain can do.
The ill I shun, the good I seek, even so
    In thee, fair lady, proud, ineffable,
    Lies hidden: but the art I wield so well
    Works adverse to my wish, and lays me low.
Therefore not love, nor thy transcendent face,
    Nor cruelty, nor fortune, nor disdain,
    Cause my mischance, nor fate, nor destiny;
Since in thy heart thou carriest death and grace
    Enclosed together, and my worthless brain
    Can draw forth only death to feed on me.

(XV)

The gist of the poem is that even the best artist is dedicated to failure, and failure means death. Neither the work of his making —the obedience of the hand to the mind, like the obedience of God's hand to His mind—nor the love of duty, will secure the immortality he so much desires. The effort of his life works to conflicting ends—he aspires to eternal life even when he is making matter into beauty, the beauty does not give him satisfaction, and the desire that drives him to create it subsides before the greater desire to unite himself with God.

He is thus as it were committed to failure, a failure that is rooted in his nature, and he asks to be pardoned. God can pardon him, and so also can a living saint, Vittoria Colonna, his friend, in her love and pity.

So much, I think, is the apparent beginning to the complexity of the thought in this poem, and only the beginning. The main point is the idea of failure, and if one asks if there is some explanation for its necessity, I think the answer that is implied is that the work of the artist does not participate fully in the harmony of ideas that are latent in the material itself with which he works. Benedetto Varchi insisted that the *concetto* of the first line was to be defined in Aristotle's terms as 'the active cause, the form that exists in the soul of the artist ... Art is nothing other than the form, that is, the model of the art object existing in the soul, which is to say, the imagination of the artist, and this form or model is the principal agent in the forming of the object'.[1]

A different reading agrees that Michelangelo in this poem is using Aristotle's theory of artistic creation, but in the form Plotinus gave it. Plotinus says in an eloquent introduction to the treatise on beauty:

Suppose two blocks of stone lying side by side: one is unpatterned, quite untouched by art; the other has been minutely wrought by the craftsman's hands into some statue of god or man, a Grace or a Muse, or if a human being, not a portrait but a creation in which the sculptor's art has concentrated all loveliness.

Now it must be seen that the stone thus brought under the artist's hand to the beauty of form is beautiful not as stone—for so the crude block would be as pleasant—but in virtue of the Form or Idea introduced by the art. This form is not in the material; it is in the designer before ever it enters the stone; and the artificer holds it not by his equipment of eyes and hands but by his participation in

---

[1] *Due Lezioni di M. Benedetto Varchi, Nella prima delle quali si dichiarà un Sonetto di M. Michelagnolo Buonarroti* (Florence, 1549), pp. 24–5. Aristotle writes most fully to this effect in the seventh book of the *Metaphysics*.

The significance of Varchi's explanation in relating *concetto* to Aristotle rather than to Plato may be judged from Panofsky's analysis of the basic issues. Briefly, the Platonic position follows from the theory that ideas in their absolute existence are immanent in matter. The Aristotelian position follows from the denial of the Ideas in this sense, and the consequent affirmation that it is the mind and soul of the artist that is the source of the idea and of the image that gives form to the object (*Metaphysics*, VII, viii [1034a4–6])—'The thing which generates is sufficient to produce and to be the cause of the form in the matter'. Panofsky presses this interpretation (*Idea*, translated by Edmondo Cione [Florence, 1952], pp. 13–17).

Varchi is deliberately denying that Michelangelo is speaking of a creative force or agent having some sort of existence prior to the poet's imagining. Despite the great weight of his authority as a friend of the poet, one is not compelled to agree with his interpretation. One must nevertheless observe that there is no reason for thinking that he was biased in favour of Aristotle, his own position in other respects being generally Neo-Platonic.

his art. The beauty, therefore, exists in a far higher state in the art; for it does not come over integrally into the work; that original beauty is not transferred; what comes over is a derivative and a minor: and even that shows itself upon the statue not integrally and with entire realization of intention but only in so far as it has subdued the resistance of the material.

Art, then, creating in the image of its own nature and content, and working by the Idea or Reason-Principle of the beautiful object it is to produce, must itself be beautiful in a far higher and purer degree since it is the seat and source of that beauty, indwelling in the art, which must naturally be more complete than any comeliness of the external. In the degree in which the beauty is diffused by entering into matter, it is so much the weaker than that concentrated in unity; everything that reaches outwards is the less for it, strength less strong, heat less hot, every power less potent, and so beauty less beautiful.

Then again every prime cause must be, within itself, more powerful than its effect can be: the musical does not derive from an unmusical source but from music; and so the art exhibited in the material work derives from an art yet higher.[1]

Valerio Mariani, having made the point of the relation of Plotinus to Aristotle,[2] goes on to say that this informing idea of the artist that Michelangelo speaks of involves his whole notion of 'the plastic conception' of the universe, and that the artist is indeed the manifestation of the very soul that Dante also speaks of, incarnate in that which circumscribes it:

[1] *Enneads*, V. 8. 1 (MacKenna's translation).

Professor Panofsky points out that Plotinus's use of the word *image*, εἶδος, signifies the object of 'an intellectual perception' in one aspect, *idea*, and in the other, *form* (*Idea*, translated by Edmondo Cione, p. 106, note 29). When Michelangelo contrasts *concetto* and *immagine* he is taking account of the relationship of the image, not merely to the conception, but to the exterior object that was the immediate occasion of its appearance. Panofsky points out that Augustine and Aquinas define image as a representation that 'proceeds from an original', and say that it reproduces what already exists. But *concetto* 'indicates the free creative representation that constitutes the very object insofar as it can by making itself into an exteriorized representation' (p. 90).

This interpretation of Michelangelo's distinction in this sonnet seems to me to go beyond what is required, and the sense Plotinus attaches to the word *image* is a clear guide to the distinction Michelangelo has in mind.

[2] Aristotle in the *Metaphysics* several times refers to what is apparently a proverb to the effect that the figure of Hermes is latent in the stone or wood. He uses the saying in developing his arguments about the meaning of potentiality. At one place, for example, he says: 'We say that a thing is present potentially as Hermes is present in the wood, or the half-line in the whole, because it can be separated from it' (IX, vi, 2 [1048a34–5]).

Michelangelo

Tosto che loco lì la circonscrive
la virtù informativa raggia intorno,
cosi e quanto ne le membre vive.

(Purgatorio, XXV, 88–90)

Now, son, expands, now distends, the virtue which proceeds from the heart of the begetter, where nature intends
all human members.[1]

I think that the interpretation Mariani gives is preferable to
Varchi's because it takes more account of the relation of the
meaning of the first lines to the rest of the poem. For some
reason not easy to understand, Varchi seems to take the first
lines out of context. One of the major points of the remainder
of the poem is that the activity of the artist does not exist in
itself, it aims towards a state of being known to God and judged
by him, and the failure of the artist is not in the failure to
realize perfectly in the work of his hands the conception within
his mind, but a failure to come into a state of being within his
mind that would be in harmony with God's purposes.

For I think one may also take the first four lines of the
poem to mean that stone contains innumerable ideas, and that
an artist can discover within himself none that are not in the
world outside him. It further says that only he—*solo a quello
arriva*—can join that which is already within him to that which
is outside and which he wishes to embrace, by working upon the
stone, when his body obeys that which grasps the idea, his mind.

[1] *Michelangelo* (Turin, 1945), pp. 167–70. Part of Mariani's interpretation
depends on his observation of a similar use of *circonscrive* by both poets in a
comparable context.

Rilke wrote a fanciful story interpreting Michelangelo's meaning, and he, too,
will have nothing of Varchi's Aristotelian explanation: '[God] bent lower, found
the striving man, looked beyond his shoulder at the hands that hovered listening
about the stone, and started: did the very stones have souls? Why was this man
listening to the stones? And then the hands awoke before him, and tore at the stone
as at a grave from which flickers a faint, dying voice. "Michelangelo," cried God in
fear, "who is in that stone?" Michelangelo listened; his hands were trembling.
"Thou, my God, who else? But I cannot reach thee." And then God knew that he
was indeed in the stone, and he felt fearful and confined' (*Stories of God*, translated
by Nora Purtscher-Wydenbruck and Herter Norton [London, 1932], p. 80).

And, again, the idea is put into a system by Focillon: 'I wish to insist ... that form
is not only, as it were, incarnated, but that it is invariably incarnation itself ...
Forms never cease to live. In their separate state, they still clamour for action, they
still take absolute possession of whatever action has propagated them, in order to
augment, strengthen, and shape it. They are the creators of the universe, of the
artist, and of man himself' (*The Life of Forms in Art*, pp. 41 and 58).

Everywhere here is the idea of authority, of what must be obeyed: it is the pressing necessity of the artist to fulfil an aim that corresponds with and harmonizes with the thought inherent in the universe. But here an idea enters that could jettison all the rest. Michelangelo does not mean to imply that there is a rational or even an engendering relationship between the universe and his own activity. He is outlining a more complex system of relationships in which something other than the thing brought into being is the end in view.

He implies now that it is not true to say that the artist works solely in the service of the image or the *concetto* that holds his mind. For he is conscious that there is something else at work, and what he achieves may fall short of his intention. Nevertheless, he must continue in his work, and if failure is the end, that too he must work for. The failure of art is not the failure of a work that is imperfect, but the failure of the work as the means of the perfection and the eternizing of the artist. What the artist seeks is not the thing, the body, the work of art, but his own truth, and his own immortality—

> but the art I wield so well
> Works adverse to my wish.[1]

And now, as the poet turns to the thought of his friend, her love for him and the strength and light it gives him, he resolves this most intricate complex of ideas. He speaks of Vittoria Colonna in words that might be beautifully applied to the Virgin—'leggiadra, altera e diva'—this beautiful lady all purity and fire, and the connection with what has gone before seems to be that just as in stone there is a truth he seeks and that seeks him, so in this mortal woman there is a parallel relation. But here, as a saint and as a woman, who inspires

[1] This is a doctrine of Plotinus: '... those drunken with this wine, filled with the nectar, all their soul penetrated by this beauty, cannot remain mere gazers: no longer is there a spectator outside gazing on an outside spectacle; the clear-eyed hold the vision within themselves, though, for the most part, they have no idea that it is within but look towards it as to something beyond them and see it as an object of vision caught by a direction of the will.

'All that one sees as a spectacle is still eternal; one must bring the vision within and see no longer in that mode of separation but as we know ourselves; thus a man filled with a god—possessed by Apollo or by one of the Muses—need no longer look outside for his vision of the divine being; it is but finding the strength to see divinity within' (*Enneads*, V. 8. 10—MacKenna's translation).

and also forgives, and more than that, who confers the last
gift, the fulfilment of his aspiration, she has the very power of
Christ, mercy and redemption.

This way of combining the ideal with the real, the spiritual
with the mortal, Michelangelo speaks of as the way of chaste love.
The terms he uses are important. It seems that the passions for
Vittoria Colonna and for Tommaso de' Cavalieri are of the
same intensity as those for his father and brothers, where also he
clings to the flesh as to life itself:

> L'un m'era frate, e tu padre di noi;
> l'amore a quello, a te l'obrigo strigne:
> non so qual pena più mi stringa o nòi ...
> Nostro intelletto dalla carne inferma
> è tanto oppresso, che 'l morir piu spiace
> quanto più 'l falso persuaso afferma.
>
> (86)

One was brother to me, and you, our father; love bound
me to him, duty to you. I do not know which burden afflicts
or troubles me more ... Our intellect is so much oppressed
by our frail flesh that death displeases by so much the more
as the flesh draws us to what is false.

Condivi remembered hearing Michelangelo say that nothing
grieved him so much after Vittoria Colonna passed away from
this life than that he did not kiss her on the brow or face as he
did kiss her hand.[1]

What all this has to do with sexuality I do not think anyone
can say, and certainly Adrian Stokes in his most discerning
analysis in Freudian terms rejects all observations of a simple
kind. Just as in the sonnet to Tommaso de' Cavalieri, where
one feels that this is as much in the tone of a Christian offering
his soul to God as it is a poem of friendship, one insists that the
power and integrity of the thought, the dignity and nobility of
the passion, are such that the reader is required to accept the
religious affirmations seriously:

> Tu sa' ch'i' so, signor mie, che tu sai
> ch'i vengo per goderti più da presso,
> e sai ch'i so che tu sa' ch'i' son desso:
> a che più indugio a salutarci omai?

[1] *Vita di Michelangiolo*, p. 94.

Se vera è la speranza che mi dai,
se vero è 'l gran desio che m'è concesso,
rompasi il mur fra l'uno e l'altra messo,
ché doppia forza hann' i celati guai.

S'i' amo sol di te, signor mie caro,
quel che di te più ami, non ti sdegni,
che l'un dell'altro spirto s'innamora.

Quel che nel tuo bel volto bramo e 'mparo
e mal compres' è dagli umani ingegni,
chi 'l vuol saper convien che prima mora.

(60)

Thou knowest, love, I know that thou dost know
   That I am here more near to thee to be,
   And knowest that I know thou knowest me:
   What means it then that we are sundered so?
If they are true, these hopes that from thee flow,
   If it is real, this sweet expectancy,
   Break down the wall that stands 'twixt me and thee;
   For pain in prison pent hath double woe.
Because in thee I love, O my loved lord,
   What thou best lovest, be not therefore stern:
   Souls burn for souls, spirits to spirits cry!
I seek the splendour in thy fair face stored;
   Yet living man that beauty scarce can learn,
   And he who fain would find it, first must die.

(LV)

Again, the Petrarchan paradox, in itself absurd, and equally absurd if referred to Freudian meanings, is anything but that if referred to the artist's faith in the absolute.

And if one relates all these intricate affirmations to his respect and passion for the physical and material, one must nevertheless not suppose that there is any weakening of the Neo-Platonic commitments. This hand or this face that is to be kissed is also in another light the embodiment of the divine. The limbs, the *belle membre*, are the reflection of something celestial:

Spirto ben nato, in cu' si specchia e vede
nelle tuo belle membra oneste e care
quante natura e 'l ciel tra no' può fare,
quand'a null'altra suo bell'opra cede:

spirto leggiadro, in cu' si spera e crede
dentro, come di fuor nel viso appare,
amor, pietà, mercè, cose sì rare,
che ma' furn'in beltà con tanta fede:
  l'amor mi prende e la beltà mi lega;
la pietà, la mercè con dolci sguardi
ferma speranz' al cor par che ne doni.
  Qual uso o qual governo al mondo niega,
qual crudeltà per tempo o qual più tardi,
c'a sì bell'opra morte non perdoni?

(41)

Choice soul, in whom, as in a glass, we see,
  Mirrored in thy pure form and delicate,
  What beauties heaven and nature can create,
  The paragon of all their works to be!
Fair soul, in whom love, pity, piety,
  Have found a home, as from thy outward state
  We clearly read, and are so rare and great
  That they adorn none other like to thee!
Love takes me captive; beauty binds my soul;
  Pity and mercy with their gentle eyes
  Wake in my heart a hope that cannot cheat.
What law, what destiny, what fell control,
  What cruelty, or late or soon, denies
  That death should spare perfection so complete?

(XXIV)

Michelangelo is not alone among the Neo-Platonists in the vitality of his *senso delle cose*, not all are like Bembo in Castiglione's *Courtier*, devoted to the etherializing of the senses. Ficino himself speaks of love and friendship in the most concrete way and with an intensity that betrays any argument he might ever offer that the flesh is but the veil of the spirit. Friendship, he wrote, 'is the enduringly honourable communion of wills. Its end is a united life. Its beginning is in knowledge, and its means is love'.[1] And again: 'The knowledge that leads to friendship is concurrence in ideas, in the stars, in the genius, and indeed in love and the affection of the body.'[2]

Michelangelo recognizes love as a power or a demon or a god—his personifications represent a sure faith. He as plainly and consistently recognizes that love moves him by the motions

---

[1] *Argumentum in Platonis Lysidem* (*Opera*, p. 1272).   [2] Ibid., p. 1272.

of the senses as much as through the soul, senses which, if they could, would captivate the soul. But he is not, I think, particularly interested in regarding the senses as the mortal enemies of the soul even though he may acknowledge their capacity to make vile. They too possess their own purity and clarity, and in the service of a 'chaste will' are themselves chaste. There is a beautiful sonnet in which the thought is articulated almost as complexly as it might be in a drama:

> Se l'immortal desio, c'alza e corregge
> gli altrui pensier, traessi e' mie di fore,
> forse c'ancor nella casa d'Amore
> farie pietoso chi spietato regge.
>
> Ma perché l'alma per divina legge
> ha lunga vita, e 'l corpo in breve muore,
> non può 'l senso suo lode o suo valore
> appien descriver quel c'appien non legge.
>
> Dunche, oimè! come sarà udita
> la casta voglia che 'l cor dentro incende
> da chi sempre se stesso in altrui vede?
>
> La mie cara giornata m'è impedita
> col mie signor c'alle menzogne attende,
> c'a dire il ver, bugiardo è chi nol crede.
>
> (58)

If the undying thirst that purifies
    Our mortal thoughts, could draw mine to the day,
    Perchance the lord who now holds cruel sway
    In Love's high house, would prove more kindly-wise.
But since the laws of heaven immortalise
    Our souls, and doom our flesh to swift decay,
    Tongue cannot tell how fair, how pure as day,
    Is the soul's thirst that far beyond it lies.
How then, ah woe is me! shall that chaste fire,
    Which burns the heart within me, be made known,
    If sense find only sense in what it sees?
All my fair hours are turned to miseries
    With my loved lord, who minds but lies alone;
    For, truth to tell, who trusts not is a liar.

(XXXVI)[1]

[1] The sonnet *S'un casto amor* (59) might be regarded as a more conventional presentation of the faith in love that outlasts bodies, and by 'chaste' he may mean simply faithful. But I think in relation to the other works, this idea here signifies that fidelity itself can purify a passion which under other conditions could lead to degradation.

So by still another path it would appear that the artist arrives again at his fulfilment in the ideal. A fulfilment and a defeat, for it begins with the furious desire to possess the stone, with the need to touch and embrace whatever is beautiful, and with the thought that what he touches he had brought into being in the first place—reversing Dante's idea of God, creating what he loved before he loved it.

And one must come at the whole process again from still another direction, for Michelangelo is also attracted by the idea that it is not only the artist, but the great intermediary, Nature, that is at work in all this. Still another dimension and another labyrinth for the mind to find itself in.

Nature is the great process in which the artist participates in his dying as in his living, but in itself it does not bring to completion the work of art. For that God's grace is needed. In the last plays of Shakespeare there is the idea again and again that art is the perfection of Nature and in that very perfection is the sign and fact of divinity—men and works alike 'grow' in grace. But for Michelangelo the arrival at perfection is the result of an intercession by God the Creator, a power and an intervention of the character manifested originally in the Incarnation.

In following his vocation Michelangelo had come to know, he said, that beauty had been given to him as an ideal. It was both a light and a mirror, leading his intellect to the very gate of heaven. All this, he concluded, was in the nature of things, and yet grace, too, was necessary to his success, in art as in contemplation—what one might take to be the nature of things was in fact so only through God's bounty:

> dal mortale al divin non vano gli occhi
> infermi, e fermi sempre pur là d'ove
> ascender senza grazia è pensier vano.
>
> (164)

> Our feeble eyes cannot raise themselves from what is mortal
> to that which is divine and remain firmly there where it is
> vain to think of mounting without grace.

The artist, by the nature of his devotion to the ideal, is caught up in the process of perfection the ideal engenders in him. The work that follows, and as a consequence of his devotion, is the work of Nature, and it is also the work of grace. It is the evidence and embodiment of his dedication.

Because the artist does think of himself as part of Nature, he likes to think of his work as Nature's way of creating life, and of abjuring death. Like Nature, the artist, too, creates something that lives—the 'immagine viva'. But whether or not this is so for Nature, for the artist the completed work does not give peace, the creation is followed by despair. Having done what he set out to do, nothing remains but death (CIX, 50).

He counters the despair by even greater ambition. He puts aside the idea of himself as the artist alone with his work, 'l'ermite esthétique',[1] to take on another role, the ruler and creator of the world itself.

Symonds called one of the sonnets a 'Prayer to Nature':

Perché tuo gran bellezze al mondo sièno
in donna più cortese e manco dura,
prego se ne ripigli la natura
tutte quelle c'ognor ti vengon meno,
    e serbi a riformar del tuo sereno
e divin volto una gentil figura
del ciel, e sia d'amor perpetua cura
rifarne un cor di grazia e pietà pieno.
    E serbi poi i mie sospiri ancora,
e le lacrime sparte insieme accoglia
e doni a chi quella ami un'altra volta.
    Forse a pietà chi nascerà in quell'ora
la moverà co' la mie propia doglia,
né fie persa la grazia c'or m'è tolta.

(230)

If only that thy beauties here may be
    Deathless through Time that rends the wreaths he
                                            twined.
I trust that Nature will collect and bind
    All those delights the slow years steal from thee,
And keep them for a birth more happily
    Born under better auspices, refined
    Into a heavenly form of nobler mind,
    And dowered with all thine angel purity.

[1] The phrase is André Chastel's, *Marsile Ficin et l'Art* (Geneva, 1954), p. 68, which he derives from Karl Borinski's *Die Rätsel Michelangelos, Michelangelo und Dante* (Munich, 1908).

Ah me! and may heaven also keep my sighs,
My scattered tears preserve and reunite,
And give to him who loves that fair again!
More happy he perchance shall move those eyes
To mercy by the griefs my manhood blight,
Nor lose the kindness that from me is ta'en!

(XXXIII)

This is in fact a claim for his own power. Nature now is such as himself, a sculptor, 'the great sculptor of men, like the Eternal in creating Adam'.[1] And he himself, the possessor of 'infinite thoughts' (286), contemplating the divine, matching the Creator, becoming what he loves, becoming God, would, one might suppose, be satisfied. But the egotism tricks him—to be like God is to conceive of God as himself. He is caught in a paradox—while he claims to imitate God, what he makes is an image of himself. He recognizes this and makes the most of it. If what he creates is himself, he might have thought of it as a rebirth, like the regeneration Ficino speaks of so finely: 'Truth dwells in the inner man ... Reasoning does not create it, but discovers it; but all the while it is there, before it is discovered, and when it is found, it renews us. Thus the inner man is reborn, and the outer wastes away day by day.'[2] In Michelangelo the same process and idea lead to another kind of rebirth:

Non vider gli occhi miei cosa mortale
allor che ne' bei vostri intera pace

---

[1] Mariani, *Michelangelo*, p. 168.
Ficino approaches the question of the relation of the form of the work of art as it exists in the mind of the artist and as it lies within the material with which he works by asserting that there is an art in Nature as in man. Nature he defines as 'ars intrinsecus', giving form and life to matter. Incidentally, for him the elements themselves possess soul (*Theologiæ Platonicæ*, IV, i [*Opera*, p. 122]). This life comes from a celestial source, the incorporeal living substance creating other substances participating in its character. The means of such creation he speaks of as seeds or as reasons (*rationes*) (to this degree he is faithful to Plotinus's conception of the origin of creation in the Logos), and the sum of this activity he calls Nature.

And then, speaking of the art of humans as an imitation of Nature, he goes on to define art *as* Nature, 'Natura quædam materiam tractans extrinsecus'. In doing this he is able to speak of art as a form of life, acting as life does, and the images in the mind of the artist through which he achieves his imitations are just such seeds and reasons of things as exist in wood or stone (III, i [*Opera*, p. 123]).

Ficino is particularly eloquent in laying out the ways in which the force we observe in art is also to be observed working in Nature and in the imagination (XVI, iii [*Opera*, p. 373]).

[2] *Theologiæ Platonicæ*, XII, v (*Opera*, p. 278).

trovai, ma dentro, ov'ogni mal dispiace,
chi d'amor l'alma a sé simil m'assale;
 e se creata a Dio non fusse eguale,
altro che 'l bel di fuor, c'agli occhi piace,
più non vorria; ma perch'è sì fallace,
trascende nella forma universale.
 Io dico c'a chi vive quel che muore
quetar non può disir; né par s'aspetti
l'eterno al tempo, ove altri cangia il pelo.
 Voglia sfrenata el senso è, non amore,
che l'alma uccide; e 'l nostro fa perfetti
gli amici qui, ma più per morte in cielo.

(105)

My eyes were not looking at any mortal thing when, looking
into your beautiful eyes, they caused me to discover perfect
peace. But I did see things such that the innermost part of
the soul, that anything evil displeases, was smitten with a
love that was proper to it, which is to say divine love. If the
soul were not created in the likeness of God it would seek
only that beauty that is external, what is pleasing to the
sight; but because it knows that beauty to be false, it turns
only to the archetype of beauty. I say indeed, that nothing
mortal can quiet the desire of that which is destined to
eternal life. More too, one cannot compare the eternal
with the temporal, with the process of time by which a
young man becomes old. The soul is killed by the desires of
the senses, for this is not truly love. The love we know
makes friends ever more perfect while they are on the earth,
but it does not make them truly perfect until after death, in
Heaven.[1]

One of the simplest ways of looking at this idea of turning
inward and the re-creation of the self is as Leonardo does,
speaking of it as what is almost unavoidable: 'A painter who
has clumsy hands will paint similar hands in his works, and
the same will occur with any limb, unless long study has taught
him to avoid it.'[2] This, too, is to be thought of as the result of
his loving what is within him—'The lover moves towards the
thing he loves as matter does to form, sense to what is sensed,

---

[1] Translated from the paraphrase of Cesare Guasti printed in the *Rime* of
Michelangelo, edited by G. R. Ceriello (Milan, 1954), pp. 211–12.
[2] *The Literary Works of Leonardo da Vinci*, ed. J. P. Richter (London, 1939), I,
342 §586.

and unites itself and becomes one with what it loves'. For the artist—'the first product of such love is the work itself'.[1]

As Leonardo puts it, although the artist becomes what he loves or aspires to, that movement of the soul that he calls love has another effect than the act of union—it produces a work. The same notion appears to be Michelangelo's. When his father died he wrote a poem to his spirit—

> La memoria 'l fratel pur mi dipigne,
> e te sculpisce vivo in mezzo il core.
>
> (86)

> Memory makes a painting of my brother, but you it sculptures alive in the centre of my heart.[2]

The figure was also Ficino's: 'Accedit quo amans amati figuram suo sculpit in animo'—the lover carves the figure of the beloved in his mind.[3]

The figures of painting and sculpture give the idea the emphases of objective reality, and they reinforce his metaphysics. For what is indeed behind all this elaborate figuring forth of the relation of the lover to the loved one, of the artist to his work, of the image Nature or grief or God carves in the soul, carves and in carving gives birth and life to, is the radical Neo-Platonic idea of the emanations of the divine, image after image in mirror after mirror. Ficino himself made the particular application: 'Thus the mind expresses (*exprimit*) and figures

---

[1] *Codice Trivulziano*, 6 r, translated from Fumagalli, *Leonardo Omo sanza Lettere*, p. 349.

As Signora Fumagalli points out, Dante says much the same thing in the *Convivio*:

> Poi che pinge figura,
> Se non può esser lei, non la può porre.
>
> (IV, x, 11)

Busnelli's note related Dante's idea to Saint Thomas, *Commentarium de generatione et corruptione*, l. I. lec. 6; *Contra Gentiles*, l. 4, c. 11; etc. (*Il Convivio*, II, 120–1).

Pico della Mirandola quoted Dante's lines to support his idea that the work of the artist is the imitation of a pattern inside his mind (*A Platonick Discourse upon Love*, 5, translated by Thomas Stanley, edited by E. G. Gardner [Boston, 1914], p. 7).

[2] This image also occurs in a letter to Vasari, when Michelangelo was speaking of his own death: 'I have come to the time in my writing when every thought I have has death sculptured within it'—'*dentro sculpita la morte*' (*Le Lettere*, edited by Gaetano Milanesi [Florence, 1875], p. 538).

[3] *In Convivium Platonis*, II, 8 (*Commentaire sur le Banquet de Platon*, edited by Raymond Marcel [Paris, 1956], p. 158). He uses it again in the *Epistolæ* (*Opera*, p. 672).

itself forth in its works, as the face of a man looking into a mirror composes the figure of himself in that mirror. And most of all an artistic mind brings itself forth into the light in words and songs and sounds. In these the entire ordering and disposition of the mind is plainly described.'[1]

But not merely *his* mind. It is also the mind of God that is figured forth, 'expressed'. And what is of particular importance for Michelangelo, all this is related to the Christan idea of the creativity of God. The Nature of the Divinity Michelangelo speaks of, who sculptures images within his mind or to whom he likens himself and his work, is not only the One of Plotinus—He is also the Maker, the Creator.[2]

Nevertheless, Michelangelo is also a Neo-Platonist, and in a way Dante was not. In this very matter of creativity and inspiration, where both men appear to use the same ideas to express their doctrines and commitments, one may perceive the dis-

---

[1] *Theologiæ Platonicæ*, X, iv (*Opera*, p. 229).

[2] Edgar De Bruyne has pointed to a remark of Athanasius for its significance in distinguishing the nature of aesthetics in Christian thought from that of previous systems: 'Often the artisan may be known from his works even when he is not to be seen, and in the same way God is to be known from the construction of the universe, whose cause and maker He is' (*Contra Gentes*, 35 [*Patrologia Græca*, XXV, 69]). Athanasius goes on to say that the order of Nature is not the order or logos of the Stoics or the Platonists (such as one may observe in Longinus), but the breath of God Himself (40). In consequence, the artist is no mere transmitter of the order of things, but the agent of God ('Esthétique paienne, esthétique chrétienne', *Revue internationale de Philosophie*, IX [1955], 130–44).

The contrast with Neo-Platonic thought may be brought out by reference to Plotinus:

'The vision has been of God in travail of a beautiful offspring, God engendering a universe within himself in a painless labour and—rejoiced in what he has brought into being, proud of his children—keeping all closely by Him, for the pleasure He has in his radiance and in theirs.

'Of this offspring—all beautiful, but most beautiful those that have remained within—only one has become manifest without; from him (Zeus, sovran over the visible universe), the youngest born, we may gather, as from some image, the greatness of the Father and of the Brothers that remain within the Father's house.

'Still the manifested God cannot think that he has come forth in vain from the father; for through him another universe has arisen, beautiful as the image of beauty, and it could not be lawful that Beauty and Being should fail of a beautiful image.

'This second Cosmos at every point copies the archetype: it has life and being in copy, and has beauty as springing from that diviner world. In its character of image it holds, too, that divine perpetuity without which it would only at times be truly representative and sometimes fail like a construction of art; for every image whose existence lies in the nature of things must stand during the entire existence of the archetype.' (V. 8. 12—MacKenna's translation).

tinction in philosophy that goes far to explain the differences in their styles. Dante's conception of the nature of love, which is ultimately the determining element in his attitude towards the work of the poet, involves an attitude towards the particular and the individual that is alien to Michelangelo. And as always with him, the reasoning behind his attitude is subtle and involved, but I think it has been fairly laid out by Kenelm Foster:

Unity is both the effect of love, since love draws things together, and the cause of love, since love is always a subject's response to some affinity, real or supposed, in an object. Unity governs love at both ends. The doctrine is traditional; but Dante's stress falls where one might have expected it less, on unity as the *cause* of love. I love most what was nearest to me before my loving began—the goodness proper to me, my 'propria bontade'.

The reason is given in a definition of love, to which the philosophical reader of Dante must continually return. Love is spiritual union, 'unimento spirituale' (*Convivio*, III, ii, 3). And union in act is meant: not only because Dante is talking about actual loving, but more deeply because all potentiality metaphysically presupposes actuality. Potency cannot, absolutely, begin anything. Without working out the metaphysics of the matter, Dante leaps to the conclusion that behind all love and desire is the perfect and perfectly actual unity or self-identity of God. Love, absolutely speaking, is God's self-identity. Hence wherever in the universe is self-identity, distinctness in nature and still more in individuality, there is love and there is a trace of God. These three terms—love, unity, likeness of God—are in this sense interchangeable.[1]

There is a certain easiness in Dante's way of seeing things, and of writing them down. He appears not to feel the necessity that Michelangelo does of marrying everything to the ideal, and although allegory and symbol are obviously his continuous concern, it is also obvious that the simply literal has for him a most serious authority. God is unique, not least in the manner of creation.

Michelangelo understood this and was in fact committed to the importance of such a view, but the extent of his commitments to Neo-Platonic assumptions prevented him from a

[1] 'The Mind in Love: Dante's philosophy', *Aquinas Society Paper* No. 25 (1956), pp. 16–17.

comparable respect for the concrete. He must concentrate on the tension in the relationship of the particular and the ideal. He will never present the thing for its own sake, the man, the armour, the veil over the face, without expressing also the mirror in which all these are the images, of ideas, of God, of himself.

In his poetry the tension shows itself in the gnarled and tortured language, the twisted conceits, the syntax that wrenches every normal procedure of reasoning in order to fashion an all but incomprehensible complexity—a word, a song of praise, a meditation, must always be identified with the self-absorption that comments on it. Yet it *is* comprehensible, the control is ultimately perfect, though the mastery is never, or perhaps never, so free and all-conquering as in his work in the other arts. But there, too, sooner or later we turn our eyes away from the David or Moses to look at the image he is giving us of himself, and of his truth—his passion and understanding and labouring. Even at his greatest he is not letting us love for its own sake the work he has made—he seems to say that even love distracts us from being ourselves and from being at peace (127).

Despite all he writes about the likeness of the artist to God, peace is not a state he can ever know. By all rights he ought to have known how to come to rest in the Ideas, as Ficino said one should, 'quiescere in ideis',[1] but the nearest thing he does know to that is what happens when he thinks about death: 'And I tell you that to rediscover and to enjoy yourself it is necessary not to seek delight and joy, but rather to think on death. It is only such thought that helps us come to know ourselves again, that holds us as it were, together, instead of letting ourselves be pillaged by relations and friends, by the powers that be and ambition and avarice and all the other vices and sins that rob a man of himself and cause him to be dispersed and dissipated.'[2] As for the bliss of solitude, this, too, turns out to be anguish. He lacks the peace of the Christians and the peace of the Platonists alike.

It has been said that 'il fut un moment où le platonisme fut intensément, profondément vécu, mêlé au rêve de tous les

[1] *Theologiæ Platonicæ*, V, xii (*Opera*, p. 147).
[2] Giannotti, *De' Giorni che Dante Consumò nel Cercare l'Inferno e 'l Purgatorio*, p. 69.

jours, en une tension presque douloureuse, dont l'effort n'était rien moins que de l'incorporer au sang et à la chair du christianisme médiéval'.[1] Such a moment was Michelangelo's life. Longinus thought of the divine vistas as joyful and serene, and I think this was possible for him because, as he saw it, the Nature he shared with all things existed in harmony and order, and he took only the slightest thought of the process in Nature that brought that order into being: Nature *was* order. He might merely say more simply, with William Blake, that all great art is praise. He was separated from the later developments of Platonism which worked together with Christianity to turn the mind inward, to see the drama of the universe within the soul, and separated also from the intolerable mystery of the Incarnation—intolerable for Michelangelo, if nearly ninety years of rivalry with God are sufficient witness of what is not to be borne. And yet his greatest works may be thought to communicate vistas as vast as those Longinus supposed the gods looked on.

For Longinus wisdom and comprehension were ennobling and sustaining, as they were for Michelangelo, for whom, however, every manifestation of the peace that truth and wisdom give was inescapably accompanied by the idea of its transience. The reasoning of Longinus appeared not to entertain the idea that anything so splendid could pass away so quickly and fearfully; he must have rested secure in the promises of his philosophy.

[1] Raymond Bayer, *Leonard de Vinci, La Grâce*, (Paris, 1933), p. 154.

MILTON

———————————

THERE IS A SENSE in which the burden of Milton's poetry
is apart from what the words and sentences say. It is as if he
were always thinking of Heaven; this is his true subject—God,
the mind of God, and the vast complexity of His truth and love
—and what he works out with words—thought, doctrine, the
delight of the senses—is but the shadow of his subject. In
Comus he is writing about the Platonic Ideas, and the masque is
the vision of a world in which forms of life are given to the
dialectic of the Ideas' existence. But the substantial matter is
something else, the zeal and purity of spirit Milton is offering
God. In *Lycidas* he is writing about the presence of the Ideas in
the mind of God, how life demonstrates their relationship to
Him, and how, in themselves and by the fact of their existence
in His mind, they are the judges of life. By a kind of reflection
the poem is about such as himself, the dedicated, but the chief
matter is Milton's promise to accept God's ways. In *Paradise
Lost* there is a similar duality. The complexity of the universe
is made to stand for the complexity of thought. Milton sets out
as it were in an exercise to demonstrate the strength and power
of the mind. He will demonstrate the comprehensiveness of
thought, able to take into its orderings even mystery and revelation, and its conclusions will manifest a form worthy of the
approbation of religion. And all this will be presented as if by
proxy, and for the rest the poem will be in praise of what is
neither ordered nor explained nor understood.

To a degree something like this is true of all art, and beauty,
power, all that moves us is something more than the poem

announces. But this other burden of Milton's is not, I think, that 'tune running in the head' Yeats said all poetry was written to, the grasp of the evanescent. With him, rather, it is what Longinus was writing of, the vista from Olympus as men imagine that to be. According to Longinus one becomes the companion of the gods—Homer and ourselves on Olympus looking down upon Achilles, Sappho contemplating the loved one as someone like a god standing beside her; but with Milton it is not so much companionship as adoration.

And there is another thing. The visions Longinus speaks of and the success of poetry in re-creating them depend on thought and imagination and virtue, and they are fiction before they are truth. Milton's vision and the success he looks for have been given to him by the processes of revelation and tradition, they are truth first and poetry afterwards. When Longinus said that in reading sublime poetry we seem to share the power of the poet and of the gods themselves, 'as if we ourselves had created the very things we see', he is arrogating a point of view and a power for the poet Milton never claims. Milton is not a mystic, and he even foregoes the power of sympathy, of putting himself in the place of the Creator. If it would be possible to speak of an attitude and a method as the opposite of Michelangelo's, it is his. The success of his poetry is in the way he stands aside, only seeing to it that reason and tradition fulfil their promises in sustaining his argument. The poetry is his own offering, something apart from the argument, the clarity and strength of his praise. In short, he classicizes.

I think what we most love in him is the continuing tone of his nobility, its sustainment under such various tests over so many years, and indeed the power for sustainment one recognized in the beginning. If one were to try to distinguish the attributes of such a quality, I suppose one would list clarity, sweetness, strength, and something best called purity, all to characterize a note that sounds in every verse, almost in every phrase. There was never a style so much a writer's own as this, never, I think, a nobility so nearly personal. What he writes of— the coming of Spring, an ancient massacre, the expulsion of the father and mother of mankind—all bear the sound of one who has given himself completely to the words that are his and only his. His initial and his final power derive from his subservience to that music, the music that must have its way, and, having that, gives him his. And he would say, is beautiful because it is an honouring of God. He never loses himself as someone who is part of the body of Christendom, or a man in a wood in the middle of his life, or someone entering the City of God. It is his own untouched, unshared integrity, a certain singleness and confidence he must always make into a style. As Milton presents it, its deepest force is in the communication of the sense of a private communion, the intensity of the inner life treasured beyond anything else. When in *Comus* Milton substituted the word chastity for charity in the triad of Christian theological virtues, he indicated not only that the virtues of philosophy might claim to be equal to those of theology, he also indicated that love for anything the world offers, even of any other soul, is not necessary for a perfected life: service to the truth of the self leads to all good. And if such is the enterprise of the soul, the style of the best poetry will accord with that, self-contained, undistracted, clear.

The style of the language of *Comus* was quickly modified. Already in *Lycidas* it is richer and the voice is so to speak a more human voice. And it became more and more resonant. But *Comus* is the beginning, and the direction Milton took there would continue to characterize what was to come later. In the *Charmides* Socrates spoke not only of the way in which each man learns to know his own truth, but also of how, in knowing it, he comes to value the truth of others, and the virtue that is the key to this knowledge belongs to the community as well as to the man. But in *Comus*, where we see the same doctrines worked out so beautifully and complexly, the strength of the argument derives from an idea of what it means to be an individual absorbed in the truth. Where Socrates was preparing to develop the argument into all the considerations that relate the individual to society, Milton rested with the individual and the way in which God might aid him in the ways of perfection. All that might intrude upon that, the sense of touch and of love and of the too-much loved earth, is sacrificed for the sake of the beauty of the doctrine. As the years pass, the poetry will reveal more comprehensive thinking and feeling, but the special strength that belongs to the particular doctrine of chastity, of individual purity, will continue to assert a dominant control.

It appears that Euripides and Tasso were two of the writers Milton most admired, writers known for their fevers and wildness and—in Stark Young's phrase—some high, complicated music in which even disease became beautiful and was called divine. Milton might say that the essential quality of poetry is to be simple, sensuous and passionate, and theirs, one might say, was more complex than simple, and with respect to the senses and passions furious or poignant. Yet it seems that there is never even an echo of this in Milton. He could not have been insensitive to the deepest and the richest power of their poetry, the decadence and torment and what transcends it, and perhaps this is one of those instances where by knowing and responding to an alien power one learns best to assure and follow one's own very different strength and beauty. Milton was the master of the enemy, and his success is in his aloofness, reordering, clarifying, by the force of the pure and single will. One cannot help but believe that in this matter he is on the side of the Counter-Reform.

The *Hippolytus* and *Bacchae* in their apparent antithesis have their occasion as much in the currents of Euripides' nature as in the issues before his civilization, and it is the same with Tasso—the consuming idea that the life of the unloved is Hell gets its terror and its beauty and its poetry from the way in which every accent of the verse weighs the poet's own experience. Milton, treating comparable matters as beautifully and sometimes, I think, as deeply, assuredly communicates the general force of his themes as well as their relationship to his own strength and purity of will and soul, but in the realm of passion, or some less clearly defined area of the spirit, one cannot be sure that as a person it would be possible for him to vouch for what the poems seem to say.

This is most notably true of *Comus*. The argument is sustained and dense in support of the claim for the magical powers of chastity—the chaste person, single in will, can by fixed purpose and adjuration overcome any hostile force the world could ever offer. However profound the doctrine, and allowing for the existence of individuals of the purest and strongest purpose, the poem does not communicate any sense that this is a doctrine that is applicable to experience generally. The conclusion—

> Or if Vertue feeble were,
> Heav'n it self would stoop to her—

lacks the sense of reality and of responsibility that are so powerfully evident in the way Saint Augustine says the same thing, that even if the body is violated, the soul of the chaste person may remain intact. Milton appears to believe that truth does not need passion to certify its authority.

Ernst Cassirer said that the Cambridge Neo-Platonists agreed with Pascal in defining faith as 'Dieu sensible au cœur, non à la raison'.[1] Nothing of the sort can be said of *Comus*—here the heart, and, indeed, passion itself are not in the province of the soul.

The charge of irresponsibility, called for by almost all Renaissance Neo-Platonism in various degrees, cannot be made so strongly against *Lycidas*. But there is a necessity to make it all the same. The analogy at the end between the rising of the sun out of the sea and Christ's ascent into Heaven, the reference also to the resurrection of Edward King, is so finely and sensitively reticent, even humbly reticent, that one accepts it as a way of affirming faith. The obvious inadequacy of the argument is not concealed, and there is no effort to lead one to suppose that this is in any sense a reasoned proof. But even so, the appeal, at this point, to 'the dear might of him that walked the waves', is an appeal that comes at the end of the poem, separate from the argument, whereas the poem itself had presented intricate reasoning about the identification of ideals with the Ideas in the mind of God, which judge each man and reward and condemn him according to the singleness of his aspiration. This is the conclusion the argument pointed to, but the gap is obvious, and the comfort fails. Even Ficino does not add enough to convince us that there is no real loss in an untimely death: 'The mind judges all things when it is with God, because it is superior to all things. And it is with Him when it understands things with complete purity, and when it cherishes what with entire clarity it understands.'[2]

Nevertheless, there has been a crucial change between the manner of *Comus* and that of *Lycidas*. *Lycidas* is informed by

[1] *The Platonic Renaissance in England*, translated by J. P. Pettegrove (Austin, 1953), p. 30 (*Pensées*, ed. Giraud, no. 283, p. 112).

[2] *Theologiæ Platonicæ*, XII, iv (*Opera*, p. 276).

love, charity perhaps, by something like passion for other than the abstract and the ideal. It may not be the love of a friend or of God that makes itself felt and that gives the poetry its weight and force, it may be more the sense of sorrow, as well as some suggestion of the fear and terror Milton felt in the loss of an ally. There may be some fear, too, of Milton's own failure. But whatever its nature, it gives the language warmth and richness, and if the result is not a style with the full weight of sympathy to support it, if it has nothing of the 'cry' of Euripides and Tasso, it is no less miraculous an achievement. There is warmth and colour in the words, the manner everywhere tells of the beauty of the senses and of feeling. In *Comus* the words are not so full-bodied—the jewel-paved streams and the asphodel for all their loveliness do not tell us so much of love and cherishing as those perfect words about Neaera and Amaryllis, the opening eye-lids of the morn, and indeed almost everything. This has more of the music of humanity.

From *Lycidas* to *Paradise Lost* the course is the course of nature. Now whatever the poet writes refers more closely to his own position in the scheme of things, the stakes are personal as well as universal, and if the power of God is still the unwavering star, there continues the sound of what is so clear in *Lycidas*, the sound that accompanies his conviction that his argument comprehends his own life. We hear the personal note almost everywhere—in Adam's questioning Raphael, in Adam taking Eve's hand, in the Father's words to the Son. And yet differently than in Dante, for example, where the poet may be thought to give all of himself to his words in order to re-create himself in every dimension, Milton gives no effect of intimacy. He works to establish more the manner than the sense of the actualities of life and conduct.

As for *Paradise Regained* and *Samson Agonistes*—to speak of them most briefly in this respect—in one the sharpness of the thought, in the other the incomparable wealth and grandeur are still closer to communicating the poet's sympathetic involvement with the general destiny of men. The sublime, the noble, the comprehensive are everywhere, but the vividness of detail that is intrinsic to Pindar and Sappho and Dante in Milton is still subdued to the general. There lacks, too, that quality of the sublime that was Michelangelo's hall-mark, the balance of violence and calm; and there lacks the beauty of passion itself, as in a mere woman's

> O sun, burn the great sphere thou movest in!

The Miltonic power and charm in the most moving passages express as little as one might think possible of the merely personal. In the splendid farewell—

> Nothing is here for tears, nothing to wail
> Or knock the breast, no weakness, no contempt,
> Dispraise, or blame, nothing but well and fair,
> And what may quiet us in a death so noble—
>
> > (*Samson Agonistes*, 1721–4)

the manner counts for almost everything, simplicity and fire and grief transmuted into quietness. The same stillness sounds in the all but intimate pathos of Satan's words when he comes to his new world:

> Is this the Region, this the Soil, the Clime,
> Said then the lost Arch Angel, this the seat
> That we must change for Heav'n, this mournful gloom
> For that celestial light?
>
> > (*Paradise Lost*, I, 242–5)

The sound, the rhythm and harmonics, suggest that every fate, the poet's also, includes the suffering of Hell, but the courage and the pride control the grief. The pathos is in the manner of Satan's patience, 'patience, the only fortitude' that is left to him. And to the reader, sounding also the poet's sense of this, it is the manner of the most resolute and elevated thought.

In its assimilative power Milton's mind is comparable to Saint Augustine's, but with Milton we do not so clearly succeed in arriving at the end to which we suppose we are being led. In true profundity, although we almost always lose our way before we come to the conclusion, we are generally confident that the road leads there. This is as true of philosophy as of theology, although even in the greatest thought there will always remain matters that are obscure or false. But the difficulty in *Paradise Lost* is not only of this kind. There is also the problem that comes from its being a poem rather than a treatise. The argument may or may not convince us, and we ask only that we can take in its implications. In Dante there are suggestions of Averroism and still other diversions from the poem's substantial scholasticism that raise serious and distracting questions. The difficulties in the thought of *Paradise Lost* are at least as troublesome—the rejection of the idea of the creation *ex nihilo*, the doctrine of God's withdrawal, ideas about the nature of substance. Difficulties of another kind are also at least as distracting, difficulties in the management of the poem itself, particularly in the matter of characterization. The confusion in the interpretation of Satan's character does not seem to me to indicate as serious an obscurity as the characterization of God the Father, or as serious as the intractable conditions of the initial situation in which it is necessary to present Adam and Eve in the state of innocence as amenable to evil.

These problems are in part like that of *Comus*—we are not led to believe that, like Macduff, the poet has felt the argument as a man who allows grief and pain their occasional sovereignty. Questions concerning verisimilitude and probability and characterization get in the way of the sense of immediacy, and in the end the terms of the author's relationship to the universe of his own creating are clearer to the mind than to the heart.

If Milton fails to present the characters in *Paradise Lost* as imaginings equal to the doctrine and religion they embody, this is a fault not in the abstract but in the art. We do not accept Michelangelo's God in the Sistine Chapel as anything but a highly personal and limited conception, but we understand the terms of the limitations. We understand them partly by reference to his philosophy and partly in the way he lets us know that this *is* a work of the imagination. Milton's God on occasion violates decorum—He fails to maintain either the traditional characterization, or the genuinely dramatic role.

The point is, I think, that Milton writes of set problems. He does not begin as Homer does, with the nature of a particular man; or as Dante, asking what is to become of himself; or as Michelangelo, acknowledging the authority of beauty and trying to square that with the sense of his own imperfection and mortality. He never does what Shakespeare always does, give nature its range. He is always academic. He approaches his matter as he does his form, as something already created, to be applied in ways that are received ways, for agreed on purposes. As far as possible he avoids invention.

Instead, what Milton chooses to do—in masque, elegy, epic, tragedy, even in the sonnets—is to harmonize a traditional form and philosophic content in a distinguished manner for the sake of the manner and everything that manner can signify as a social and generalized form. He does this with such high purpose, such perfection of taste and intelligence, that the result achieves the sublime in precisely the sense that Coleridge indicated—'In the Paradise Lost the sublimest parts are the revelations of Milton's own mind, producing itself and evolving its own greatness; and this is so truly so, that when that which is merely entertaining for its objective truth is introduced, it at first seems a discord'.[1] It is the wholeness of such a mind Coleridge is emphasizing, encompassing 'boundless or endless allness',[2] and the sublimity is partly in the vista and partly in the quality of the poet's mind. The thought is again Longinus's, the noble mind seeing the world in the way someone very like a god would see it.

The academic spirit in the Renaissance glorified the superhuman. The learned were not merely to be the companions and advisers of princes, they were the oracles of antiquity. They might present themselves as schoolmasters and as members of the Republic of Letters, but the function and manner were aristocratic and lordly. Taken in a certain spirit, as by a man like Vittorino da Feltre, humanism made education and scholarship a divinely sweet and charitable calling. In a spirit only less wonderful, it made learning a grand and proud profession, so sure of itself it could claim to supplant the hierarchy of breeding and rank with that of excellence and brilliance.

For the humanists magnificence and generosity of mind characterized the idea of the poet, as one who might address kings. One sees something of this in Spenser and Du Bartas in their ways of emulating the ancients. Milton would have seen such lordly aspirations close to in his travels in Europe, entertained in the great cities by persons of the highest rank, in Rome by a Prince of the Church. He would have noticed how

[1] R. F. Brinkley, ed., *Coleridge on the Seventeenth Century*, (1955), p. 578.
[2] Ibid., p. 596.

these stamped the achievements of music and opera and architecture. Reading his own verse to members of an academy in Florence he would have met style with style, elegance with elegance. He would have fulfilled the role.

But what came through his own achievements was still something else—clarity above all; no stress would be permitted to darken the clarity either of his vision or his feeling. It is the abiding characteristic—in a poem on the coming of Spring, in the intricacies of image and syntax and rhythm in the poem on the Nativity, in the Ovidian wealth and easiness of the praise of Nature. It is the note of strength, of the clear, strong soul, and this inextricably part of his conception of the nature of the poet himself, in his character as a man of the most honourable and virtuous sort—the note of the singly dedicated continues to dominate: 'he who would not be frustrate of his hope to write well hereafter in laudable things, ought himself to be a true poem'.[1]

The adoration, then, of a man whose character itself is a poem, the life of praise—this might apply to the work of a number of the best artists, and of course the elements are fused differently under different circumstances. Each man's style is his own, the ring of his mind is only his, and there are, too, I think, preoccupying images or something still more general than an image that provide him with a constant subject apart from the immediate burden of his different works. It is this that Coleridge points to in Milton: 'I can understand and allow for an effort of the mind, when it would describe what it cannot satisfy itself with the description of, to reconcile opposites and qualify contradictions, leaving a middle state of mind more strictly appropriate to the imagination than any other, when it is, as it were, hovering between images. As soon as it is fixed on one image, it becomes understanding; but while it is unfixed and wavering between them, attracting itself permanently to none, it is imagination. Such is the fine description of Death in Milton:

> The other shape,
> If shape it might be call'd that shape had none
> Distinguishable in member, joynt, or limb,
> Or substance might be call'd that shadow seem'd,

[1] *An Apology for Smectymnuus* (*The Student's Milton* [New York, 1934], p. 549).

For each seem'd either; black it stood as Night,
Fierce as ten Furies, terrible as Hell,
And shook a dreadful Dart; what seem'd his head
The likeness of a Kingly Crown had on.[1]

(Paradise Lost, II, 666–73)

And such, I think, is the character Milton sets upon his thought and language equally.

Professor Hanford once observed that in the First Prolusion, 'Whether Day is more excellent than Night', a mention of morning and the joy it brought raised the writing to the beauty of *L'Allegro* and *Comus*,[2] and indeed it seems that the idea of morning, if one may call it that, was always to draw on the central life of Milton's imaginings and thoughts. It is not only that in image after image his poetry achieves a special vividness and power when this is his subject, but from time to time the mention of morning seems to include the idea of Paradise, it seems to embody the clarity that belongs to the soul as it does to the world. Whether one regards this as an archetypal image or not, it assuredly influences his imagining in his most sustained work as well as in single lines, providing, it seems, some part of the impulsion and indeed the power and authority of what it means to gain or lose Heaven. If one puts aside the theory of archetypes as not proven, one must still believe that as an image, and perhaps as an idea, morning kindled Milton's thought to the point that it led him into the most extensive and significant elaborations. And if one considers what his poetry for the rest tells us, that it is in adoration that he writes, that it is God he is always praising, then this would happily enough be an immediate means of speaking about the God of Light. And if this is not to be named as an image, archetypal or otherwise, it may be regarded as a conception, in the term Longinus used, enthralling the imagination and sounding the intrinsic quality of his mind.

There are many occasions to show how in the earliest poetry Milton drew on this power, most elaborately, of course, in the *Ode on the Morning of Christ's Nativity.*

In the beginning stanzas we are told of the blazing light of

---

[1] *Coleridge on the Seventeenth Century*, p. 594.
[2] *John Milton* (New York, 1949), p. 37.

God darkened in its entering a mortal body, and the hymn that follows is offered as a present to 'the approaching light'. The hymn itself begins with a scene of the world in the rule of winter, a Christless world, and at night. It has been a long night, and it is now late, and, as happens almost always before dawn, stillness and peace seem to come over everything, as if to prepare for some mysterious event. And just as naturally as the growth of brightness, this quietness is accepted as an image of the heavenly peace which stills the war and lust of the benighted world.

The wind dies down, the waves grow calm, and even the stars take on an expectant quiet. Time for a moment seems to have stopped, and the sun hesitates. Only the shepherds at the very point of dawn keep chattering, ignorant of the wonder that is to come. Then even they heard the music that was in the stillness. Then the light came and a great splendour filled the world and the music of the awakened life of the earth sang as it had never sung before, in harmony with the music of the spheres and the angels.

For a moment it seemed that the golden age was about to return, with Truth and Justice and radiant Mercy, but this was only a foreshadowing and a promise, time must run its course, the sun will rise and the Infant God must grow to complete His task. This morning's dawn will give way and neither peace nor justice will come to the earth yet, but the harbinger of bliss speaks the truth and the dark divinities know it, hiding in their twilight thickets like shadows fleeing from the sun.

And now day comes in its full power and the chariot of the new star that has risen in the sky is ready to attend the Lord when He awakens.

The conception the poem follows is that the beatitude of morning foretells the dawn of Christ.

In *L'Allegro* there is the same wonder to begin the poetry, the freshness of dawn on a May morning. In the Epilogue to *Comus* Aphrodite waits for the moment when Adonis is to awaken in the gardens fair; and Cupid and Psyche, at the time foreseen by Jove, are to rise from their entranced embrace to the eternal light. In *Lycidas* there is the same miracle of a morning's promise, 'the opening eye-lids of the morn'. Here the promise is of love and truth and of Christ, a promise that overcomes the misery of evil and that supports the life of those who survive to enter other pastures on still another morning:

> So sinks the day-star in the Ocean bed,
> And yet anon repairs his drooping head,
> And tricks his beams, and with new-spangled Ore,
> Flames in the forehead of the morning sky.
>
> (168–71)

Milton referred to the Nativity Ode in the sixth elegy, addressed to Charles Diodati, and acknowledged that it was indeed the light of dawn that inspired the poem:

> Dona quidem dedimus Christi natalibus illa
> Illa sub auroram lux mihi prima tulit.
>
> (87–8)

> This is my gift to the birthday of Christ,
> the first rays of its dawn brought the theme to me.[1]

The coming of morning gave the beginning to the story he tells in the Seventh Elegy:

> Ver erat, & summæ radians per culmina villæ
> Attulerat primam lux tibi Maie diem:
> At mihi adhuc refugam quærebant lumina noctem
> Nec matutinum sustinuere iubar.
> Astat Amor lecto, pictis Amor impiger alis ...
>
> (13–17)

> It was spring and shining o'er the roofs of the houses, the light had brought to thee, O May, thy first day; but my eyes still sought receding night and could not endure the brightness of dawn. Beside my couch stood Love, tireless Love with iridescent wings.

This is, of course, the very subject of *On May Morning* and it becomes even more richly coloured in the poem on the Fifth of November:

> Jam rosea Eoas pandens Tithonia portas
> Vestit inauratas redeunti lumine terras;
> Mæstaque adhuc nigri deplorans funera nati
> Irrigat ambrosiis montana cacumina guttis.
>
> (133–6)

---

[1] Translated by Nelson G. McCrea in *The Student's Milton*.

Now rosy Tithonia, opening the portals of the Orient,
clothed the earth with the gold of the returning light, and
still lamenting the sad death of her swarthy son, she bedews
the mountain heights with ambrosial drops.

In the wonderful poem *On the Coming of Spring* the inspiration
of Apollo takes the poet into the fields of light, into the very
temples of the gods, where he sees as they see:

> Jam mihi mens liquidi raptatur in ardua cœli,
>   Perque vagas nubes corpore liber eo.
> Perque umbras, perque antra feror penetralia vatum,
>   Et mihi fana patent interiora Deûm.
> Intuiturque animus toto quid agatur Olympo,
>   Nec fugiunt oculus Tartara cæca meos.

(15-20)

Now my mind is swept away into the heights of the clear sky
and through the wandering clouds I move released from
the body; through the shadows I am borne on and through
caverns, those sanctuaries of poets, and the inner shrines of
the gods lie open to me.

The ecstasy leads into the sublime vista itself.

When Edoardo Coli proposed that the substantial conception
of the *Vita Nuova* was the image of the Earthly Paradise, that it
was out of this that all that related to Beatrice took form, we
are repelled, I think, by the notion that anything other than
the love of a person was the beginning of that work. And when
he went on to suggest that it was this same image with its
deepening power over him that was the origin of the *Divine
Comedy* itself, we are even more doubtful that this is so because
that work so surely leads from all sides to another object than
the creation of a scene. There the idea of salvation quite
transcends the beauty of even the loveliest places in the
universe and the poem becomes primarily a poem of persons
and of God conceived as a person.

If one were to propose something as simply as this for
Milton, that the idea of morning was not only a special incite-
ment to his imagination but was indeed the genial conception
of all his work, this would be as much as to say with Petrarch that
the end of thought is clarity. From wherever Milton began he
would be led into the praise of light, his imaginings supported

by all the ideas that accrue to that, from Saint John and Plato
and the Platonists, leading into the most complex metaphysics—

> Hail holy light, ofspring of Heav'n first-born,
> Or of th' Eternal Coeternal beam
> May I express thee unblam'd? since God is light,
> And never but in unapproached light
> Dwelt from Eternitie, dwelt then in thee,
> Bright effluence of bright essence increate.
>
> (*Paradise Lost*, III, 1–6)

The life of fame within the mind of all-judging Jove, the vision
of the sainted seats and of God upon His throne, the panorama
of the universe, would be limited by the character of the idea of
morning. For Milton there is nothing of mysticism in this—at
most there is the conviction that the light of the mind is the light
of God, and of the world. All would be conceived as 'a beatific
vision and as a natural outgrowth of life on the human level'.[1]

If one stopped at this point in supposing any such matter to
be the centre of Milton's poetry, one would think his final
effect would be, so to speak, of unpeopled glory. If this is his
substance, it would seem not to allow for individual personages
as among the chief forms of the creation. It cannot be so
simple, and yet by the nature of Milton's art and I suppose of
the cast of his mind, individuals are not at the centre of his
imagination. With Milton the end is never as it is with Dante,
the poetry of the individual as an individual. Except for Satan
and the characters of *Samson Agonistes*, it is precisely the persons
who fail to come to life. God, of course, is ever present, but more
as truth and love and power and justice than as a figure of the
imagination. As for the poet's own image, it comes to us in the
sense of his nobility and greatness, not as someone on a journey,
harried and passionate and marked by experience. It comes to
us as 'the ring of a noble mind', the nobility of thought and of a
character which is itself a poem. The poetry no more than the
theology looks towards the proclamation of the incarnate, but
rather towards 'the effluence increate'.

Serge Eisenstein, the film director, observed somewhere that
the structure of *Paradise Lost* was conceived as it were cinemato-

[1] M. Y. Hughes, 'Milton and the Source of Glory', *Philological Quarterly*, XXVIII
(1949), 115.

graphically, and the insight is remarkably instructive. It corresponds in many respects with what Miss Marjorie Nicolson has said about the effects of Milton's interest in astronomy, and for the present purpose it appears to accord with all that I would like to say about the power of the idea of morning and of light. More important still, it offers a way of seeing how such a conception in its expression in the conduct of a poem leads into the realm of meaning.

Looking at the poem in this way, one observes that after the announcement of the subject and the invocation—what brought man to his present state? Who is the serpent, who is the fallen angel that led man to turn from God?—the camera focuses on Hell, on the arrival of the angels at their last home. There they take stock of the situation, debate the future, and decide on war. But before taking action Satan decides to explore the universe. He traverses the extent of Hell, passing through its gates and through Chaos and its vast space to the shores of the Earth.

Then the scene of the poem changes. Now we are in Heaven, with God looking down upon the regions of the world, watching Satan in his great journey. After God tells His Son what is happening, pointing Satan out to him, and tells Him of what the future is to bring, the Son accepts the idea His love for man directs him to. There is then great rejoicing in Heaven, and suddenly the camera changes again. Now we see Satan landing on the Earth, and then, after a brief reconnaissance, he returns to Hell.

That narrative is now discontinued, and the scene becomes an intimate one. The camera focuses on the humans who have been the occasion of all that the poem has so far narrated—the story of the casting down into Hell, of the dialogue at the throne of God, of the journey of Satan into space. There is now something like a close-up: Adam and Eve are leading their quiet lives, they entertain a guest, Raphael, who explains much they care to know about their lot and the Creation. The conversation takes in elaborate descriptions of the universe but this is partly done in order to intensify the intimacy of the group in the Garden.

There then follows a succession of events in which changes of scene follow rapidly one after another. Satan comes to the

Earth, as a vapour and as a serpent. The Guardian Angels ascend to Heaven to report on what has happened on the Earth, Christ descends there for the judgment He must give, Sin and Death construct a great bridge to connect Hell with Earth. Satan returns to Pandemonium and the congress of angels become serpents, Michael and other cherubim move towards the dispossession of Eden, and Michael leads Adam to a hill to offer a look into the future and to emphasize the Resurrection. The poem ends with the father and mother of mankind hand in hand leaving Paradise on their long journey, and the last words give us the image of them the whole poem was preparing for from the beginning—a sight all the other rangings through space and time explained—

> They hand in hand with wandring steps and slow,
> Through *Eden* took thir solitarie way.

This technique of ordering the succession of scenes is a way of fulfilling that early aspiration—'fana patent interiora Deûm'. It is more powerfully controlled in the epic than in the *Ode on the Nativity*. Or than in *Comus*, which, beginning with the descent from Jove's court, became a demonstration of the mingling of worlds within the soul, and passed finally into an apotheosis. In still another aspect this way of ordering the imagination defines the progress of *Lycidas*. It is the characteristic manner of Milton's putting things together, and as such it demonstrates again what Coleridge said of Milton's greatest achievements, that they are the revelations of his own mind, 'producing itself and evolving its own greatness'—juxtaposing vistas for the sake of their final focus on the state of the soul of man, where the images of light drive out the dark; the imagination 'unfixed and wavering', as Coleridge said it is when it is most truly itself.

In *Lycidas* the moving back and forth between heaven and earth is controlled by the circumstances of the poem in a more than usually complex way. By the nature of the poem, as reflections brought to bear upon a single incident, it shows one of the most significant qualities of the way Milton's imagination works in the praise of God. For here the love of truth and of the light of truth is stamped with the detachment that properly belongs to those who undertake to praise justice, who are faithful enough to praise the justice of God. It is this, I think, that accounts for the balance in his imagining between the general and the particular, and the quality of his language in which what is visualized stops short of the clearest and most concrete images even while its clarity and application are unmistakable.

The place of the poem is the imagination. The laurels and myrtles the poet addresses in the first lines are not real, they exist only in his thought. The landscape in which he thinks of them, the river close by, whatever he calls it, is inhabited by nymphs and sea gods as he cares to think of them and with whatever qualities he wishes to give them. And indeed, all the circumstances that he takes such pains to describe and to localize, he imagines simply in order to bring out the central conditions of King's life. And it is because the poem begins in this obviously imagined situation that it must never leave that sense of the fictional, of the unreal, even though what Milton is speaking of is serious enough. And so when Milton has Saint Peter speak and although what he says has the most immediate relevance to actual circumstances in the life around Milton, almost the first detail is a false one, an imagined one—the river Alpheus shrinks—and the obscurity of the allusions, and the allegories, continue to keep our thoughts at a distance from the circumstantiality that would break into the consistency of the world of the imagination that provides the original conception of the poem.

But if the poem has no particular use for circumstantiality, allowing only a minimum of reference to the facts that have occasioned it—the imagining, nevertheless, is not presented as something irresponsible and fantastic. It does deal with truth and with reality, philosophically conceived or, if one likes, poetically conceived. The point of view with which the poem begins is the point of view of a poet imagining and not portraying, but conscious that he is imagining; selecting his images, commenting about them, introducing into them interpretations and ideas, and maintaining consistently a certain detachment and a certain critical evaluation of those very things that his imagination is calling up and ordering. In his imagining he relates that a good man has died, and he asks how this can be permitted by a just God. He provides an answer, in appealing and in part arguing to the doctrine of the Resurrection. But the point to be made is that the poem does not begin as something imagined and then turn into a presentation of faith or a theological argument. The point to be made about *Lycidas* is that it is perfectly consistently conceived, that the imagining of the beginning is an imagining which involves detachment and judgment. And the conclusion of the argument, that this man has not died uselessly, that he will be rewarded in Heaven, that God is indeed just, that He does not repay His faithful servants with injustice, all this is contained in the early statement—

> *Fame* is no plant that grows on mortal soil,
> Nor in the glistering foil
> Set off to th'world, nor in broad rumour lies,
> But lives and spreds aloft by those pure eyes,
> And perfet witnes of all judging *Jove*.
>
> (78–82)

He says here that what a man does and the real value of what he does exists in the mind of God. It exists as something seen 'by pure eyes', and the very sight of it in the mind of God is at once its eternizing and the very judgment that God puts upon it. Milton means that one should act in the perfect confidence that justice will be done. One will act knowing that what one does will become a part of the mind of divine justice and will take up its life in that mind eternally.

In saying so much, the poet is saying that the dialectic of his imagining is itself a confirmation of the existence of justice. The way of imagining in conforming to general truth is the very way of justice, the way God might see.

It was a considerable part of Professor Tillyard's purpose to show that Milton's poetry revealed a progression of thought towards an ever more definite discipline: 'Milton's mind ... presses forward to some end. He will have none of what does not subserve his purposes. Power, order, stability must come first, and sensibility be sacrificed if need be. Thus we saw how Milton deliberately narrowed, as he grew older, the comparatively varied sensibility shown in the Nativity Ode.'[1]

---

[1] *Milton* (London, 1930), p. 358.

The point is, I think, that as Milton passes from *Comus* and *Lycidas*, after the long interval, to the greatest works, his mind, taking in so much more of the complexities of the world as of thought itself, was by that fact committed more and more deeply to serve the truth, the truth the ordering of his thought attested. The imagination comes increasingly to serve the uses of reason. The language of his expression would be formed according to the respect he owed to logic and reason, to truth and justice, and there would be little enough of what he owed to his special sensibility.

Somehow he created the language he needed, a language to show the balance he had achieved in his imagination between the claims of the general and the particular, between the philosophical and the concrete, a way of transforming that almost Ovidian richness into the Doric delicacy—that old epithet of Mackail's is the right one, as characteristic of the later as of the earlier temperament. Milton is his own witness in affirming that the love of truth determined his choice of words:

For me, Readers, although I cannot say that I am utterly untrain'd in those rules which best Rhetoricians have giv'n, or unacquainted with those examples which the prime authórs of eloquence have written in any learned tongu[e], yet true eloquence I find to be none, but the serious and hearty love of truth: And that whose mind so ever is fully possesst with a fervent desire to know good things, and with the dearest charity to infuse the knowledge of them into others, when such a man would speak, his words (by what I can expresse) like so many nimble and airy servitors trip about him at command, and in well order'd files, as he would wish, fall aptly into their own places.[1]

He was less explicit in the passage on eloquence in *Paradise Regained*, but there he spoke of

> swelling Epithetes thick laid
> As varnish on a Harlots cheek.
>
> (IV, 343-4)

In the abstract such statements mean all or nothing. Where they become useful is when we relate them to what Milton takes to be the truth, what grand scheme his observations lead

---

[1] *An Apology against a Pamphlet call'd A Modest Confutation*, etc. (*Complete Prose Works*, ed. D. M. Wolfe, I [1953], 948–9).

him to affirm. And about this one ought to be able to say something, to characterize to a degree the features of his language that are determined by a way of looking at the world that must have remained constant, and by a view of the order of the universe his knowledge supported. A study of what he meant by 'Nature', for example, and how he uses words to describe Nature, will help us understand what he means by 'truth' and how truth serves the imagining of God's ways.

The significant passages in Milton's prose which reveal his attitude towards Nature are consistent in affirming that Nature is in essence a principle of being, and, more specially, of coming into being.

[Nature] means either the essence of a thing, or that general law which is the origin of every thing, and under which every thing acts.[1]

When Milton directed his attention to the process rather than to the principle of growth he tended to regard the informing force of Nature as a physical or even plastic power. There is a hint of this in a remark which refers to the theory of the war of the elements.

For if we look but on the nature of elemental and mixed things, we know they cannot suffer any change of one kind or quality into another, without the struggle of contrarieties.[2]

What from one point of view is regarded as law in Nature, from another is the principle that informs creation, and even the creation of souls:

It would seem, therefore, that the human soul is not created daily by the immediate act of God, but propagated from father to son in a natural order.[3]

Nor is there any reason to suppose that the influence of the divine blessing is less efficacious in imparting to man the power of producing after his kind, than to the other parts of animated nature ... whence in Scripture an offspring is called *seed*, and Christ is denominated *the seed of the woman*.[4]

[1] *The Christian Doctrine*, translated by C. R. Sumner, Bk. I, ch. 2 (*The Student's Milton*, p. 923).
[2] *The Reason of Church Government Urged Against Prelaty* (*The Student's Milton*, p. 520).
[3] *The Christian Doctrine*, Bk. I, ch. 7 (*The Student's Milton*, p. 979).
[4] Ibid., Bk. I, ch. 7 (*The Student's Milton*, p. 979).

At one place, at least, in *Paradise Lost*, the ideas of law and of generation are identified, and the 'contrarieties' of elements derive from the very life in the pregnant elements:

> this wilde Abyss,
> The Womb of nature and perhaps her Grave,
> Of neither Sea, nor Shore, nor Air, nor Fire,
> But all these in thir pregnant causes mixt
> Confus'dly, and which thus must ever fight,
> Unless th' Almighty Maker them ordain
> His dark materials to create more Worlds.
>
> (II, 910–16)

Such a notion is not far from a personification of Nature in the manner of Scève, Ronsard, and Du Bartas, but in Milton it is generally less passionate and less confused:

> The Earth obey'd, and strait
> Op'ning her fertil Woomb teem'd at a Birth
> Innumerous living Creatures, perfet formes,
> Limb'd and full grown.
>
> (VII, 453–6)

Professor Greenlaw once summed up the nature of this conception of the universe in a way that helps relate all this to Milton's choice of words:

The constant use of the old physics,—the realm of Chaos and Night, the war of the elements, the description of Hell as a universe of death where Nature, perverse, breeds monstrous things; his account of the abyss, the womb of Nature and perhaps her grave, are a few of the many examples that might be cited. His interest is physical, not biological.[1]

It is, I think, necessary to qualify this last sentence, to say that a 'biological' interest easily follows an awareness of the physical nature of things, and no less than the 'physical' it offers a systematic way of translating the impressions of the senses into the orderings of thought. The trick is in the balance—in philosophy, by the terms with which Milton can relate the physical to the spiritual; in poetry, by the control of the language of the senses through the ideas, the 'truth', that leads the words to fall into 'well-order'd files'. A balance such as these lines speak of and demonstrate:

[1] Edwin Greenlaw, 'Spenser's Influence on *Paradise Lost*', *Studies in Philology*, XVII (1920), 326.

O *Adam*, one Almightie is, from whom
All things proceed, and up to him return,
If not deprav'd from good, created all
Such to perfection, one first matter all,
Indu'd with various forms, various degrees
Of substance, and in things that live, of life;
But more refin'd, more spiritous, and pure,
As neerer to him plac't or neerer tending
Each in thir several active Sphears assignd,
Till body up to spirit work, in bounds
Proportiond to each kind. So from the root
Springs lighter the green stalk, from thence the leaves
More ærie, last the bright consummate floure
Spirits odorous breathes: flours and thir fruit
Mans nourishment, by gradual scale sublim'd
To vital Spirits aspire, to animal,
To intellectual, give both life and sense,
Fansie and understanding, whence the soule
Reason receives, and reason is her being,
Discursive, or Intuitive.

(V, 469–88)

The order that controls the words is the order that Milton's idea of the scheme of Nature presents him with. The words, or most of them, are predetermined by the scheme and their historical use in the development of that scheme. What for the sake of style and distinction and interest Milton allows himself to add, are in the devices of amplification, an occasional inversion or synecdoche—in short, embroidery. The first and last thing is in the statement of the fact, and in the outline of the scheme that certifies its factuality.

Milton's descriptions of the force of Nature differ in the intensity of their sensuousness, and in general it appears that the intense use of sensual imagery varied directly as he emphasized the teleology of Nature. For instance, in the quite objective transposition from *Genesis* of the description of the creation of plants, the language which speaks of the earth as a mother is almost simply ornamental:

Let th' Earth
Put forth the verdant Grass, Herb yeilding Seed,
And Fruit Tree yeilding Fruit after her kind;
Whose Seed is in her self upon the Earth.

112

He scarce had said, when the bare Earth, till then
Desert and bare, unsightly, unadorn'd,
Brought forth the tender Grass, whose verdure clad
Her Universal Face with pleasant green.

(VII, 309–16)

But in the important passage on the moment of Creation, in
which Milton describes the germinal force in things, the
imagery is intensely sensual:

Thus God the Heav'n created, thus the Earth,
Matter unform'd and void: Darkness profound
Cover'd th' Abyss: but on the watrie calme
His brooding wings the Spirit of God outspred,
And vital vertue infus'd, and vital warmth
Throughout the fluid Mass, but downward purg'd
The black tartareous cold infernal dregs
Adverse to life.

(VII, 232–9)

These varied expressions of the nature of things and of the
force that informs and controls them all tend towards personification. This is as one might expect from that key invocation at
the beginning of the third book of *Paradise Lost*. What is in the
first instance a plea for inspiration by the divine light is also a
definition of what Milton understands to be the nature of the
life of the universe, a statement so carefully expressed it supports
the materialistic physics of the poem at the same time that it
affirms the idea of the teleology of things:

At the opening of Book Three in *Paradise Lost* the conception
receives consummate expression. Here 'form' no longer is the
purpose that shapes, or the soul that inhabits this or that particular
body, but the spirit that, having its effluence from God, produces His
created universe. Availing himself of the associations of Biblical
usage, and probably inspired by the Neoplatonists and Dante,
Milton now calls this essential spirit *light*, and identifies light, form,
and essence ...

To the imagination of Milton, then, light is the manifestation of
the heavenly spirit, the first of things, the quintessence pure, the
bright effluence of bright essence increate. Since light emanates
from Divinity, it carries with it wisdom and holiness; and the progress of all forms toward perfection is made evident by their capacity
to receive light. In these lines, with their vivid directness and beauty,

we have the classic expression of Milton's belief in the interrelation of essential and visible condition.[1]

From one point of view it hardly matters what philosophy one relates this to. Taken as the expression of materialism, it yet remains a celebration of the force of life, of a materialistic pantheism:

> For know, whatever was created, needs
> To be sustaind and fed; of Elements
> The grosser feeds the purer, earth the sea,
> Earth and the Sea feed Air, the Air those Fires
> Ethereal, and as lowest first the Moon;
> Whence in her visage round those spots, unpurg'd
> Vapours not yet into her substance turnd.
> Nor doth the Moon no nourishment exhale
> From her moist Continent to higher Orbes.
> The Sun that light imparts to all, receives
> From all his alimental recompence
> In humid exhalations, and at Even
> Sups with the Ocean.
>
> (V, 414-26)[2]

From still another angle, it has been argued that Milton derived his idea of the creation as the effect of the moving of the Spirit of God upon the face of the waters from Hebrew writers on *Genesis*:

... Ben Gerson conceived of this Spirit as having been present at Creation in at least two aspects, one of which was Wisdom ... and the other as Understanding ... Through and by means of the presence of these two Spirits, or these two manifestations of the Holy Spirit of God, there was continuously revealed God's 'gift' to Chaos, or to the stuff of Creation. This gift, the presence of Wisdom, was the quality of becoming perfected or receiving the quality of form to a certain degree through the process of Creation. This process consisted of the revelation of the presence of God's Spirit in the Universe ... The revelation of Wisdom and Understanding or plan in the Universe was the real process of Creation.[3]

[1] Ida M. Langdon, *Milton's Theory of Poetry and Fine Art* (New Haven, 1924), pp. 17–18.

[2] This is an argument of Denis Saurat, *Milton, Man and Thinker*, (New York, 1925), pp. 303–5.

[3] H. S. Fletcher, *Milton's Rabbinical Readings* (Urbana, 1930), p. 131.

In short, Milton's idea of Nature and its laws and life is so complex that several interpretations may be thought to be at least partly valid. All of them have something to say about what he considers to be the truth of things, the guide he proposes to enable him to form the language he requires as a poet writing in 'the hearty love of truth'. And all of them indeed might be thought to be subservient to the principle of ordering facts clearly, the single-hearted faithfulness to the things themselves, and the clear relating of the things to the 'scheme', the simple, clear scheme.

The words that present and describe the order of things, Milton says, fall easily into place. I suppose he means that when knowledge takes in the extent of God's order, and all is articulated according to reason and understanding, then the words one uses—to name particulars and to show their relation to the whole—fall into place because the place has been prepared for them by the very systematization of what they express. (Just as Lycidas takes his place in God's order by the very fact of his being seen by Him.) And to the degree that the words belong to a received vocabulary, of poetry or philosophy or science or theology, the poet's task is that much more easily accomplished, the light of truth being both his guide and his subject.

We may judge something further of what he means, I think, from the passage in which he describes the source of the light of the planets and the stars. He is drawing our attention not only to a system and a religious idea, but also, most vividly, to the facts themselves:

> Of Light by farr the greater part he took,
> Transplanted from her cloudie Shrine, and plac'd
> In the Suns Orb, made porous to receive
> And drink the liquid Light, firm to retaine
> Her gather'd beams, great Palace now of Light.
> Hither as to thir Fountain other Starrs
> Repairing, in thir gold'n Urns draw Light,
> And hence the Morning Planet guilds his horns;
> By tincture or reflection they augment
> Thir small peculiar, though from human sight
> So farr remote, with diminution seen.
>
> (VII, 359–69)

To this passage the old editor Todd supplied a parallel in Lucretius:

> Largus item liquidi fons luminis, aethereus sol,
> inrigat adsidue caelum candore recenti.
>
> (V, 281–2)

The greatest charm of Milton's description is, perhaps, in the suggestion of a scene in Biblical or classical literature, with the images of golden urns and palaces and the temple of the sun, but in another respect the chief effect of the passage is to emphasize the fact of the physical nature of light. Milton in greater detail than Lucretius was describing a phenomenon, not merely developing a conceit or laying the groundwork of a metaphor. The notion of the sun as a fountain of light depended on the idea that light was a liquid. The figure, 'the Morning Planet guilds his horns', obtains its literal force from the same notion.

Milton also says that although the sun, 'the Fountain', is the giver of light to other bodies, it is not the primary source of light. Light was first taken from the 'cloudie Shrine' and placed in the sun's orb. This is the way it is in *Genesis*—God created light and divided it from darkness on the first day. He did not create the sun, moon, stars and planets until the fourth day. Milton is both repeating and justifying the account of *Genesis*. Sir Isaac Newton does much the same thing, and if the language has less colour it is no more specific or schematic:

... one may suppose that all ye planets about o^r sun were created together, there being in no history any mention of new ones appearing or old ones ceasing. That they all, and ye sun too, had at first one common chaos. That this chaos, by ye spirit of God moving upon it became separated into several parcels, each parcel for a planet. That at ye same time ye matter of ye sun also separated from the rest, and upon ye separation began to shine before it was formed into that compact and well defined body we now see it. And the preceding darkness and light now cast upon ye chaos of every planet from the solar chaos, was the evening and morning, wch Moses calls ye first day, even before ye earth had any diurnall motion, or was formed into a globular body.[1]

---

[1] Letter to Dr Thos. Burnet, *c*. 1681 (Sir David Brewster, *Memoirs of the Life, Writings, and Discoveries of Sir Isaac Newton* [Edinburgh, 1855], II, 451).

The sun which 'drinks' the liquid light, and is in turn a source or fountain of light for other heavenly bodies, plays a part in Milton's description of the universe not very different from the one Newton described in referring to an 'aether in the aether':

And as the earth, so perhaps may the sun imbibe this spirit copiously, to conserve his shining, and keep the planets from receding further from him: and they that will may also suppose that this spirit affords or carries with it thither the solary fuel and material principle of light, and that the vast aetherial spaces between us and the stars are for a sufficient repository for this food of the sun and planets.[1]

Whereas Milton was in agreement with Newton in the general idea of a 'nutriment theme' in the universe, he tended to emphasize the sun as the source of light to a greater degree than Newton. But in emphasizing that, he was consistent with his other descriptions of the sun as the very heart of the system of nature.

> they [Constellations] as they move
> Thir Starry dance in numbers that compute
> Days, months, and years, towards his all-chearing Lamp
> Turn swift their various motions, or are turnd
> By his Magnetic beam, that gently warms
> The Univers, and to each inward part
> With gentle penetration, though unseen,
> Shoots invisible vertue even to the deep.
>
> (III, 579–86)

The elaborations of thought as well as the precision of the language make it evident that there is a body of complex and detailed reasoning behind such statements, and that the language is accurate not only in a sense agreeable to a materialistic view of things but also in reference to ideas of a more obviously animistic or teleological kind. Even when the imagery is primitive and literary it never introduces ideas that go counter to Milton's real knowledge. For example, he is careful not to say that the vital power of the sun is the sole factor in the creations of Nature—he emphasizes equally the necessary fecundity of the earth. He does this, on occasion, in vivid personifications:

[1] Letter to Oldenburg, January 25th, 1675/6 (Brewster, I, 394).

> while now the mounted Sun
> Shot down direct his fervid Raies to warme
> Earth's inmost womb.
>
> (V, 300–2)

The idea the image depends on is the same as that the sun is the
source of light and of life, and the personification commits
Milton to no view of things that contradicts his conception of
the nature of the physical universe. It is a partly valid extension
of the way in which he regards the relations of the four elements,
in their nourishing and supporting of each other; and what is
not, strictly speaking, rationally valid, is not demonstrably
invalid:

> of Elements
> The grosser feeds the purer, earth the sea,
> Earth and the Sea feed Air, the Air those Fires
> Ethereal, and as lowest first the Moon;
> Whence in her visage round those spots, unpurg'd
> Vapours not yet into her substance turnd.
> Nor doth the Moon no nourishment exhale
> From her moist Continent to higher Orbes.
> The Sun that light imparts to all, receives
> From all his alimental recompence
> In humid exhalations, and at Even
> Sups with the Ocean.
>
> (V, 415–26)

The personification is but another manifestation of a system of
ideas that explains the workings and the life of Nature in all its
forms:

> Aire, and ye Elements the eldest birth
> Of Natures Womb, that in quaternion run
> Perpetual Circle, multiform; and mix
> And nourish all things, let your ceasless change
> Varie to our great Maker still new praise.
> Ye Mists and Exhalations that now rise
> From Hill or steaming Lake, duskie or grey,
> Till the Sun paint your fleecie skirts with Gold,
> In honour to the Worlds great Author rise,
> Whether to deck with Clouds the uncolourd skie,
> Or wet the thirstie Earth with falling showers,
> Rising or falling still advance his praise.
>
> (V, 180–91)

Milton mingles the images of mythology and religion with the observations of science but always in serving the presentation of the truth. The figures of the imagination, the metaphors, the myths, the personifications, express in part facts also discoverable to reason, and they also express, by their very reference to life, the idea of divinity that belongs also to the things of the universe itself. All is God's work, reflecting or sharing in His life.

The point should perhaps be emphasized by another illustration.

Milton several times, explicitly or by implication, referred to the warring elements, but only once is the Nature outside Chaos said to be in a state of war, and in this instance Satan is deliberately using the terrors of Nature to subdue Christ.[1] This one considerable description of a war in Nature manifestly uses terms of the old science as poetic imagery, and does not represent Milton's conception of the true nature of elemental processes. For Milton, as for Newton, Nature was a 'perpetual circulatory worker', but except when he said that the light of the sun is given to the stars by 'tincture or reflection' he was not explicit in his terms that describe the processes of circulation. The exhalations and mists of the earth rise and rain falls, but he does not say that the whole is a process of distillation. He says only that elements nourish each other. But the two notions are closely related and a comparison of a similar idea in a contemporary writer may serve to set off Milton's conception:

> For heat, the begetter of vapours, is no where wanting: so that the World is nothing else but a great Vaporarie, or Stove. For the earth doth alwayes nourish infinite store of vapours in its bowels: and the sea boiles daily with inward vapours, and the air is stuft full of them every where. And we shall see hereafter, that the skie is not altogether free from them. But living bodies of Animals and Plants, are nothing but shops of vapours, and as it were a kind of Alembecks perpetually vaporing, as long as they have life or heat.[2]

He stops short in theory as he stops short in the exploitation of sensibility.

When Milton did describe the processes of Nature in the

[1] *Paradise Regained*, IV, 397–431.
[2] J. A. Comenius, *Naturall Philosophie Reformed by Divine Light: or, A synopsis of Physicks*, Englished by an unnamed translator (London, 1651), p. 101.

image of the sun's rays fertilizing the earth, he did not develop the personification as it might have been done, into a personification of the elements themselves. He held back. In Milton's most intense personification of the earth, when, as Eve plucked the apple,

> Earth felt the wound, and Nature from her seat
> Sighing through all her Works gave signs of woe,
> That all was lost,
>
> (IX, 782–4)

for all the audacity of the figure, the violence of the upheaval is played down. It is not Milton's purpose to emphasize what might overwhelm our feelings. The important emphasis is to another effect—the result of sin is 'the *deforming* of the world'.[1] The order of reason was disturbed, the order that was the object of all thought, the substance of all art. Milton directs the effect of the most terrible moment in the poem not to our feelings but to our understanding. It is through understanding that man shows his own divinity, and from the reader at this point Milton also demands the noblest and most elevated comprehension.

Milton does not challenge divinity—he admires, adumbrates, and serves. The force of his intellect, the revelation of the power of his mind, this is the achievement one puts beside the efforts of Dante and of Michelangelo to rival the Creator, and to undertake the very work of creation. The ambitions of Milton are obviously human, and the effects of his poetry are neither ecstasy nor transport. There is neither the mysticism of the *Paradiso* nor the *terribilità* of Michelangelo. But if the word sublime does refer above all else to the power of understanding, as I think it does in Longinus, a power inherent in the universe as in man, then Milton deserves the term again and again.

[1] Langdon, *Milton's Theory of Poetry*, p. 15.

INDEX

Index

Dickens, Charles, 38
Diogenes Laertius, 12n.
discretio, 31-2, 35
Dodd, C. H., 10
Dodds, E. R., 15n.
Dolce stil nuovo, 33
Donatello, 58
Donne, John, 41
Doré, Gustav, 47
Du Bartas, Guillaume de
   Saluste, 98, 111

Ecstasy, x, 1, 5, 6n., 9, 16, 17,
   120
Eisenstein, Serge, 104-5
Enthusiasm, 3, 7n.
Epicurean philosophy, 12n.
Epinomis, 9
Euripides, 38, 93, 95

Farinelli, Arturo, 71n.
fastigiositate, 35n.
Ferrero, G. G., 63n.
Ficino, Marsilio, 7n., 52, 61n.,
   62n., 63n., 65, 66n., 70n., 71,
   79, 83, 85, 88, 94
Fletcher, H. S., 114
Focillon, Henri, 58, 75n.
Foster, Kenelm, 87
Fumagalli, Giuseppina, 63n.,
   67n., 85n.
Fyfe, W. H., xi, 11

Garin, Eugenio, 52, 65
Genesis, x, 112, 116
Giannotti, Donato, 62, 88
Girardi, E. N., 53n.
Gorra, Egidio, 22-3
Grace, 68-70, 81
Greenlaw, Edwin, 111
Grube, G. M. A., xi
Guasti, Cesare, 53n., 84n.

Hamlet, 11

Hanford, J. H., 100
Heracleitus, 8n.
Hermetic philosophers, 10
Hippolytus, 93
Hollanda, Francisco de, 51n.
Homer, ix, x, 2, 4, 5, 7, 10, 16,
   91, 97
Howell, A. G. F., 30n.
Hughes, M. Y., 104

Ideas, 13, 73n., 88, 90, 94
Imagination, 11, 12, 14n., 107
Imitation, 11, 15, 83n.
Incarnation, 48, 49, 75n., 81, 89
Inspiration, 6-11, 15n., 16, 32,
   33, 34, 35, 37-8, 50, 51, 54n.,
   86, 113

Kant, Immanuel, x
Kissling, R. C., 14n.
Klein, Robert, 15n.
Kristeller, P. O., 7n.

Langdon, I. M., 113-14, 120
Laws, 11n.
Leonardo da Vinci, 63n., 67n.,
   84, 85
Logos, 33, 83n., 86n.
Lomazzo, Antonio, 54n.
Longinus, ix, x, xi, 1-17, 28, 29,
   35, 37, 48, 49, 51, 57, 61, 86n.,
   89, 91, 98, 100, 120
Lorenzo delle Colombe, 62
Lucretius, 116

Mackail, J. W., 109
Manzoni, Alessandro, 31
Marcel, Gabriel, 15n.
Mariani, Valerio, 74, 75, 81
Marigo, Aristide, 32n., 35n., 36n.
Marmion, Shakerly, 43
Mazzeo, J. A., 32n., 33n., 37n.
Medici, Cosimo de', 52
Medici, Lorenzo de', 52

Index

Vittorino da Feltre, 98

Wicksteed, P. H., xi, 32n.
Wolfson, H. A., 15n.

Yeats, W. B., 91
Young, Stark, 93

Zeno, 11n., 14n.